UNDERSTANDING OURSELVES

Why we do what we do

by

Christine Corbett

MADION PRESS
Sussex
MP

Printed and Bound in Great Britain by:
The Cromwell Press Ltd
Wiltshire

Madion Press
Sussex

A CIP catalogue record for this book is available from the British Library.

ISBN 0-9551111–0–2

This book is dedicated to my children,
Madeleine, Damion and my husband Jeff,
without whose help it would not have been possible.

Contents

Acknowledgements

I am grateful to Professor Kevin Connolly and Dr Margaret Martlew for permission to take quotations from their book *Psychologically Speaking*

Cover Art designed by Damion Corbett

Cover head design used by permission of Malcolm Thain

Illustrations by Jeff Corbett

Inkblots created by Christine Corbett

Preface

The aim of this book is to acquaint the lay reader with the most interesting aspects of human development.

In our lives we go through many different stages. Good things happen to us and so do bad.

Hopefully this book will offer insight into our psychological make-up and how this can affect our relationships with other people, both close to us, and strangers in the outside world.

Fictitious case histories are used to illustrate the material discussed and real dreams have been interpreted.

Most of the knowledge we have about people's behaviour is the result of scrupulous research, which includes conducting experiments under laboratory conditions and using statistics to assess people's behaviour. Psychologists also observe human behaviour in the natural environment and take case histories from individuals, of their own unique experiences. I have used the major theories and latest psychological research available in an attempt to explain why we do what we do and how we react to certain situations by examining how our minds are working at any particular time.

The theories of Sigmund Freud are very heavily criticised for being untestable. They are the product of small scale studies of Jewish middle-class women living in Vienna at the turn of the century and his own personal self-analysis. Despite Freudian theory being heavily debunked and being subject to the whim of psychological fashion, it is still as strongly debated as it was when it was first conceived in Victorian times.

The large array of therapies available for people experiencing anything from a lack of confidence, to highly debilitating nervous disorders, is a big contrast to what was available at the turn of the century. Humanity has progressed from chaining the 'deranged' to asylum walls. Subjecting the brain to electric shocks, and the indiscriminate use of "chemical strait-jackets" (the tranquillizers and anti-depressants highly favoured in the 1950's and 1960's), have been replaced by a more humanistic approach to the treatment of psychological problems.

An understanding of the processes we are going through in our everyday lives can make it easier to cope when we experience problems.

APES & US

The human race has been divided into three classifications: the Negroid, who is of medium height, heavy build and who has a protruding lower jaw and thick lips; the Mongoloid, who has facial features adapted to cope with the cold (that is a small bridgeless nose, eyes protected by layers of fat in the lid and generally flat features); and the Caucasoid group, to which both Europeans and Asians belong, which is characterized by a long heads, a bridged nose, varying skin colour and thin lips.

It is believed that all human beings originate from a single set of ancestors who lived in Africa 150 thousand years ago. These are thought to have been the dominant hominid species on the planet for 5,000,000 years.

General belief has it that around seven million years ago the "Southern Ape", which had previously been living in the tropical forests of Africa, moved to the plains. These Southern Apes had different characteristics; some were slender, and others more stockily built, and they walked upright.

Possibly their migration to new territories in search of food for themselves and their offspring created the phenomenon of invention, i.e. tool making and the use of weapons for hunting animals, etc, which in turn created further evolution.

In 2000, scientific journals reported on research carried out in Sweden which suggested that all modern human beings were descended from less than 10,000 ancestors.

A scientist called Eric Lander believes that present day Europeans are direct descendants of a few hundred Africans who migrated 25,000 years ago.

In 2002 an Oxford scientist, Bryan Sykes, claimed in *"The Seven Daughters of Eve"* that most European people alive today could be traced back to seven female ancestors.

The very first ancestor of humans, speculated to be "The Missing Link", was discovered in Chad in Africa in 2002 and was nicknamed "Toumai", meaning, "Hope Of Life". It is believed to be between six and seven million years old.

In 1974 Donald Johanson discovered the remains of "Lucy", who belonged to a species which is believed to be 3.5 million years old. Present day humans are thought to have evolved from "Lucy".

An American anthropologist called Jensen, some 30 years ago, claimed in his book *"The Origins of Races"* that different races had evolved at different rates. He believed that the White and Oriental populations had evolved more rapidly towards modern humanity than Africans and Aborigines. However, his theory has been dismissed by the results of genetic analysis. In-depth scientific research has shown that there is actually more variation between people of the same race than people of different races.

Our closest relatives in the animal kingdom are believed to be the Bonabas or Pygmy chimpanzees who live in the rain forest of Zaire. These creatures are very elusive and are thought to have a genetic makeup that is 98.4% similar to that of human beings. They have a system of verbal communication, establish friendships and indulge in face-to-face copulation which is comparatively rare amongst non-human primates. Sexuality plays an important part in the development of hierarchies within their community.

The ability to communicate our thoughts with language is something which is unique to human beings. Human language has

16 features that distinguish it from uttering sounds and pointing, or using sign language.

The nearest a chimpanzee has come to using spoken language is "Vicki" who in 1951 managed to utter the words "mama, papa, cup and up" – possessing only the verbal abilities of a one year old child.

Sign language has been used in an attempt to discover the extent to which chimpanzees can communicate in language.

"Nim Chimpsky", (a pun of on the name of a Psychologist called Noam Chomsky - a leading name in the study of language), was selected from intelligent parents to test whether it was possible for chimpanzees to communicate with words. Nim was reared like a human baby by researchers Stefanie Le Farge and her husband. Nim wore nappies, was played with and cuddled, could crawl by two months and was pot trained by 12 months. He would also scream for his bottle or dummy. He was trained in AMESLAN (American Sign Language) – and learned his first sign at four months (the same age as deaf children). He was also able to communicate with his feet. In four years Nim learned 125 signs. He also learnt learned to combine signs such as "tickle-me", "more-eat", and produced 5235 distinctly different signs, but was not able to progress into constructing sentences. The longest communication that Nim was able to utter was "give-me-orange-me-give-eat-orange - me-eat-orange-give-me-eat-orange-give-me-you". The project ended when Nim was four years old because of financial constraints.

Other researchers worked with a female chimpanzee called "Washoe", again with American sign language. After three years training she knew 85 signs and after 5 years she could communicate with 160 different signs. Washoe then went to live

3

in a chimps colony run by Roger Fouts. A chimp in this colony was able to translate the spoken word into sign language. A female gorilla also devised her own form of swearing by making sign language for "you dirty big toilet".

It is thought that human beings have an inbuilt Language Acquisition Device – LAD for short. It is possible that language originated in cave dwellers as a series of grunts which acted as a communication source for mating. In modern times language has romantically sexual connections in the form of poetry, songs and literature. There is no doubt that the ability to convert thoughts, particularly abstract concepts, into verbal communication is unique to our species.

Chapter 1

OUR PERSONALITY TRAITS

"The phrase nature and nurture is a convenient jingle of words for it separates under two distinct heads the innumerable elements of which personality is composed"
Francis Galton (1822-1911) The Human Faculty

Are body shape and personality related?

Throughout history attempts have been made to associate physical appearance with personality.

William Sheldon described three body types which he called somatotypes, and which he believed were associated with certain personality characteristics. He described:

- *the ectomorph,* who is thin, delicate and lightly muscled and who is brainy, self-conscious, private and mentally overactive;

- *the mesomorph,* who is rectangular and muscular and has a desire for power, combined with aggression;

- *the endomorph,* whose body type is soft and round in build and has a love of food and comfort possessing a relaxed and tolerant nature.

Young schizophrenic patients tend to have a predominantly ectomorphic body build. Delinquent boys too, in detention centres, have been found to show a high degree of mesomorphy.

Another attempt to associate physical build with character was made by Kretschner who described three distinct types of people:

5

- *the "pycknics"*, who are broad, fat and short and tend towards depression;

- *the "asthenics"*, who are thin and tend to be schizoid;

- *an intermediate group of muscular people* with a more stable mental make-up.

Research has shown that people generally believe that a sallow complexion denotes hostility; blonde hair – goodness and virtue; wrinkles around the eyes – good humour and friendliness; old age – maturity and wisdom. Women with a high forehead and who wear glasses are generally deemed to be intelligent. Thick lips are believed to signify sexiness; thin lips – non-sexiness; and bowed lips – conceit, immorality and a demanding nature.

Large noses have been associated with arrogance and dominance and people having small noses are believed to be submissive and feminine. John Lavator wrote in 1872: "firm lips = firm character; weak lips = weak character". A lipless mouth resembling a single line denotes coldness, industry, love of order and precision; if drawn upwards at the two ends, this can be a sign of affectation and pretension. Large eyes are thought to promote warm feelings in humans and animals, and this is believed to protect them from aggression – both babies and the young of animals have eyes that are very large in relation to their head size.

Aristotle stated that a high forehead was a sign of intellect and intellectual pursuits are usually described as "high brow" although there appears to be little evidence to prove this is the case.

Brain maps

Franz Joseph Gall was a distinguished anatomist who pioneered research into the brain in the 1800's. He helped establish phrenology, and claimed that there were 27 organs in the brain each of which were responsible for a particular mental function and the better these functioned, the larger they were, and the more they affected the overall shape of the skull.

Peoples' character traits were determined by examining the shape and configuration of the skull, and phrenology was popular in the 19th century. Phrenology has now been discredited in the 20th century with the introduction of sophisticated technology to perform brain scans.

A Phrenologist's map of the brain

An accurate map of the brain reveals a different picture to that painted by phrenologists and these have been achieved by "Magnetic Resonance Imaging", "PET" and "CAT" scans.

7

A Psychologist's map of the brain

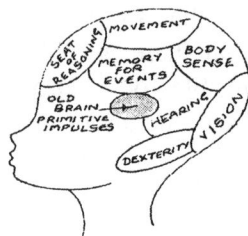

The human brain weighs 3-4 lbs and contains 100 billion nerve cells. The cortex is the outer layer which is grey matter and is the "computer element" of the brain, while the old brain deep in the centre houses our primitive impulses of sex, hunger, thirst, anger and aggression. It is speculated that it may contain the "seat of conscience".

The brain is divided into two hemispheres, left and right. The left hemisphere is mainly responsible for verbal ability and the right hemisphere for tasks using shape and form. The right hemisphere controls the left side of the body and many artists, architects and sports people who need a highly developed awareness of shape, form and accuracy tend to be left-handed. Many top tennis players such as John McEnroe, Goran Ivanisovich and Jimmy Connors are left-handers. As the right hemisphere of the brain is also responsible for producing negative emotions, this could account for the temperamental behaviour displayed by some left-handed sportspeople.

Luigi Godda, Director of the Gregor Mendel Institute in Rome, has suggested that left handed people are more likely than right-handers to become alcoholics, psychotics, epileptics and dyslexics and are prone to immune disorders. However, left-handers are more likely than right-handed individuals to be gifted, particularly at mathematics.

Looking at our self-concepts

One important aspect of personality is our concept of *"Self": Who am I?*

The *"whole self"* as described by Abram Maslow is acquired by satisfying needs.

The most basic need that a person has is the physical need to be warm and to satisfy hunger and thirst. Next is the need to feel secure and out of danger. Higher up is the psychological need to belong and to be loved. People then need to have knowledge and understanding of the world around them. They have increasingly more sophisticated needs which are to see and appreciate beauty.

The highest need, which can only be met when all the preceding needs have been satisfied, is *self-actualisation;* the ability to reach one's full potential. Self-actualisation is achieved by people who are able to take chances and try new experiences. These people tend to take their own advice and do not rely on authority. They are generally honest, hard working and responsible and have the confidence to hold unusual or unpopular views. Richard Branson is a well known self-actualiser, who, it is believed, began his career by buying and selling records from a public phone box and who is now head of a multi-million pound conglomerate. It is obvious that a strong component of achieving self-actualisation is believing in yourself.

The role we play in life will affect our self-perceptions. They provide a sense of identity *'who I am'* and they give us a clear public identity to adopt. Problems often arise when people find themselves in roles they dislike but cannot change. This may take the form of disliking one's job or profession but being unable to make a change for the better. Adopting one desired role such as being a mother can often automatically incur another role e.g. housewife.

"All the world's a stage, and all the men and women merely players"

William Shakespeare
1564 - 1616

We are all actors in the drama of life; social actors with strict standards for these roles and we must act our parts well to feel comfortable in these roles. We often hide behind our roles, distancing our real selves from the roles we play.

Psychologists believe that people tend to have favourable evaluations of features that relate to themselves. Beauty is seen to be more important than brains when we are beautiful but unintelligent.

When other people are unfavourable to us we tend to apply our defences. People who criticise us we tend to ignore, discredit or disbelieve. If we realise that someone doesn't like us we evaluate them in a negative way to reduce their status and prevent damage to our self-image.

The "self" is sometimes managed and presented differently from the way a role is acted. Clothing and home décor, according to E. Goffman, are forms of self-expression, free from the constraints of role expectation.

People are believed to maintain their self-image by two main strategies. Firstly, we perceive and interpret external events and then protect ourselves by misperceiving negative information. For example, if we love someone, we may pretend the love is returned when in reality it may not be. In order to further to protect our self-image, we mix with people of similar backgrounds, levels of intelligence and attitudes.

If we have negative characteristics we are likely to project them on to other people, in order to protect our own self-perception.

Personality labels

Galen, an ancient Greek physician, elaborated on an existing idea that personality traits could be separated into four categories. He described these as the four temperaments or humours which are based on the bodily secretions of the person, for example, bile from the liver.

- *Melancholics* are inward looking and emotionally volatile.

- *Cholerics* are outgoing and emotionally volatile.

- *Phlegmatics* are inward looking and emotionally stable.

- *Sanguinics* are outgoing and emotionally stable.

Hans Eysenck, in the 1950's and 1960's, described what he claimed to be inherited personality traits.

He described extraverts and introverts, who could be either stable or unstable.

11

- *Stable introverts* are reasonable, highly principled and controlled.

- *Unstable introverts* are worried, suspicious and thoughtful.

- *Stable extraverts* are playful, easygoing and sociable.

- *Unstable extraverts* are hot headed, quickly aroused and active.

He believed extraverts in general have poor concentration and easily become bored. Stable extraverts enjoy high levels of stimulation and are likely to be sportspeople. They do better at primary levels of education than at secondary levels or in higher education. Unstable extraverts often have criminal tendencies.

Eysenck felt introverts to be more socially conforming; their brains are naturally more aroused and they are more sensitive to noise and pain. Stable introverts are likely to be scientists, mathematicians and business people. Unstable introverts do well in higher education and at university but are likely to be neurotic.

Hans Eysenck believed that heredity plays a vital role in the production of individual differences. He cited studies of adopted children being more like their natural parents, whom they have never met, than like their adoptive parents. Studies of identical twins reared apart have shown them to be more similar to each other than their adoptive parents. More recently genes have been identified for skills, talents and I.Q.

Eysenck also created a scale of "tough-minded/tender-minded" individuals. Tough-minded people would tend to hold views such as "ethnic minorities are too powerful"; support the death penalty; have strongly conventional religious beliefs; and are likely to be highly patriotic. Tough-mindedness is found predominantly in people who suffer schizophrenic disorders. The crimes of the tough-minded criminal are mugging, GBH and sex crimes.

Eysenck blamed permissiveness for the increase in violent crime in the Western world. He also claimed that the wearing of tattoos has a strong link with violent criminality. Tattooing is very similar to the war paint worn by primitive tribesmen, and it could be that people who have tattoos are giving off a "warning signal" to other people that they are a force to be reckoned with.

The tender-minded people described by Eysenck tend to hold liberal views; are radically minded; often being pacifists; supporting easier divorce and abortion; are anti-racist; and are anti-sexist. These people may well have stronger egos than tough-minded people and life may generally have been kinder to them, lessening their need to be so ego defensive.

Once a criminal, always a criminal?

An anthropologist called Lombrosso, who lived in the 19th century, believed that criminals were a separate species who had not evolved in the same way as "normal people". He called them "Homo Delinquens" and believed they were genetically half way between modern man and his primate ancestors.

He claimed to have identified a stereotype of criminals who were described as having a flat nose, large ears, fat lips, a large jawbone, and high cheek bones. These people were believed to have a liking for tattoos and cruel games. He suggested that they had their own language, some type of primeval slang.

Criminality was claimed by Eysenck to be an inherited personality trait and not a product of social conditioning. He painted a picture of the criminal personality – a caricature of an unstable extravert who is resistant to social conditioning, strongly emotional (neurotic) and of whom it can be said that three quarters of his personality is inherited. The identical twin of a criminal is apparently four times more likely also to be a criminal than his brother who is not genetically identical. Eysenck claimed that environmental improvements such as better education and housing have failed these people because they are genetically programmed for criminality.

Eysenck believed that it was difficult to cure criminals and quoted studies carried out in both the USA and the UK that seemed to show that psychoanalytic therapy failed to cure persistent offenders. Research has shown that 63% of boys who have criminal fathers become criminals themselves.

However, there are cases of people who had previously been hardened criminals being rehabilitated and changing their lives. John McVicar came from the East End of London and served a long prison sentence for the crimes he committed. Whilst in prison he studied and achieved a Masters Degree in Sociology and on release into the community became an author and journalist.

Jimmy Boyle came from the East End of Glasgow and committed serious crimes for which he was imprisoned. Whilst serving his sentence he studied art and on release married and became a sculptor exhibiting in many galleries.

It appears that men have more antisocial tendencies than women. Statistically men are three times more likely than women to be dependent on alcohol and drink heavily. They are also more likely to use illegal drugs. Men are believed to commit 95% of crime and form 96% of the prison population.

New research claims to be able to identify criminal tendencies in children as young as 4 years and this has been related to brain abnormalities which can lead to criminal behaviour in later life. This is known as "Attention Deficit Conduct Disorder", or AD/CD for short, and is characterised in childhood by a lack of normal feelings and emotions. Deliberate anti-social acts are poorly connected with guilt and remorse in these children and they have little emotional restraint for being cruel. They also tend to be compulsive. Apparently the type of home environment these individuals are born into appears to play very little part in influencing their behaviour and discipline tends to have little effect.

Over half the people having been identified as having AD/CD were arrested for crimes before the age of 18 years. Many of these people have violent traits. Medication to increase the level of stimulation to the frontal regions of the brain has proved to be effective in reducing anti-social behaviour by increasing its ability to be influenced by behaviour restraining emotions.

A list of symptoms that precede this disorder has been constructed; this is "inconsequential behaviour" beginning in childhood.

- Starting off other children off in scrapping or rough play.

- Being careless, untidy, losing or forgetting books and pens.

- Being slapdash.

- Not being able to concentrate for long.

- Not knowing what to do with his or herself and not being able to stick at anything for long.

- Being too restless to remember anything for long.

- Needing constant petty corrections to schoolwork.

- Being inclined to fool around in team games.

- Getting involved with foolish pranks and gangs.

- Showing off and pulling silly faces. Taking the 'micky' and clowning around in general.

- Slumping and lolling around a lot.

- Flying into a furious temper if provoked.

- Being resentful, muttering and making insulting remarks.

This behaviour tends to be more common in boys than in girls and children who tend to score highly on this list also tend to score highly on tests designed to measure 'maladjustment'; this relates to children of eight years old and over.

Researchers also believe that children who are born more than two weeks prematurely or two weeks post-term are more likely to score highly on tests of maladjustment than children born on their expected delivery date.

The Psychopath

The psychopathic person is egocentric, hostile, aggressive and selfish, seeking personal gratification above all else.

More recent research into psychopaths has shown them to have superficial charm, be pathological liars, be manipulative, have shallow personalities and lack the ability to relate to other people's feelings. They also tend to be prone to boredom and to be impulsive. They often have a "parasitic" lifestyle, living off other people.

It is believed that psychopaths may have faulty brain wiring. Damage to a small region of the frontal lobe of the brain has been associated with severe anti-social behaviour, particularly rage attacks. A small area of the brain, called the amygdala, is believed to be responsible for producing appropriate emotional responses to other people's distress. Damage to this area is thought to be associated with psychopathic behaviour.

Research carried out with psychopaths has shown that they display very low anxiety levels in fearful situations and therefore they would not avoid anti-social behaviour for fear of the consequences. As lie detectors measure a person's emotional responses to questions, it is possible that a psychopath could beat the 'lie detector test'. Fear of punishment can be a powerful tool in controlling a child's behaviour and it may be that psychopaths have avoided being socialised at an early age.

The overriding feature of the psychopath is that they appear to be entirely lacking in any form of morality. Various reasons have been given to explain the cause of psychopathic behaviour. Lack of maternal affection in childhood is one of the factors cited – they are "depraved because they are deprived".

"Moral imbecile" was a term originally applied to psychopaths by the Mental Deficiency Act of 1927 and was later named "moral defective". The psychopathic personality type could be applied to all varieties of psychological abnormalities, but specifically to people who could be described as explosive, affectionless and weak willed.

The Serial Killers

The examination of the brains of some serial killers has shown various degrees of damage, but not all display abnormalities. In the case of Fred West, the serial killer who also murdered his children, both explanations are relevant in that it is believed he was sexually abused by his mother and then later sustained head injuries in a motorcycle accident.

The serial killer Ted Bundy is believed to have killed over 30 women, possibly more, in an extremely brutal and sometimes sexual manner.

His early childhood was dysfunctional. Born in 1946, he was illegitimate and raised by his grandparents whom he believed to be his parents. He shared the same house as his mother believing her to be his sister. At the age of 23 he discovered the true nature of his family situation.

Bundy came across as a very charming and educated man. He also had a Psychology Degree. After his mother's remarriage he was treated very well by his stepfather, who tried to bring him up as his own son. Bundy also had three step-siblings.

Experts studying his case found no evidence of psychosis, neuroticism, alcoholism or addiction to drugs. Neither did they find what they believed to be character disorder, amnesia or sexual deviation.

However, they decided that Bundy had a strong dependency on women and that this dependency was abnormal. He had a strong fear of being humiliated in his relationships with women. As a teenager he was involved in petty crime such as shoplifting.

The GP, Harold Shipman is believed to be Britain's worst mass murderer. He was born in Nottingham in 1946 and his mother died of lung cancer when he was 17. It is believed that after starting work as a GP he became addicted to pethidine which is similar to morphine. Although he was convicted of only 15 murders and forging a will, it is estimated that he killed at least 262 people, most of his victims being women.

Shipman was both arrogant and vain. He was married with four children and lived what appeared to be a normal family life until his arrest, imprisonment and subsequent suicide in 2004.

Does the environment help shape our personalities?

In contrast to this Michael Watson stated many years ago:

"Give me a dozen healthy infants, well formed and my own specialised world to bring them up in and I'll guarantee to take any one at random and train him to be any kind of specialist I might select – Doctor, Lawyer, Artist, Merchant and yes even beggar man/thief regardless of his talents, penchants, tendencies, abilities, vocations and race of his ancestors".

Watson believed that all children were born with "tabula rasa" – a blank state of mind on which anything could be written. He believed that the environment was totally responsible for shaping a person's personality.

Most theorists today, whilst acknowledging the undoubted contribution of genetics to an individual's personality make-up, also give credit to the influence of the environment. It could be argued that it is politically and socially dangerous to attribute a person's character traits totally to their gene pool. This happened in the 1920's when research seemed to indicate that personality characteristics were inherited and an organisation called known as the British Eugenics Society called for the compulsory sterilisation of people they described as "alcoholics, perverts, delinquents and the feebleminded".

Although it has been shown that there is a very strong case for the influence of heredity on a person's make-up, the effects of the environment cannot be ruled out, particularly in relation to intelligence and general behaviour. Research with children has shown that by improving their general environment, significant improvements can be made to their characters.

Freud's ideas on how our personalities develop

Professor Sigmund Freud, a household name, has probably contributed more to the science of Psychology than any other person.

He was born in Moravia, Austria in 1856 and his work and theories led to the opening up of entirely new avenues of psychological thought and the foundation of a School of Psychoanalysis. Freud originally trained as a Clinical Neurologist. From 1902 to 1938 he was Professor of Neurology at Vienna University. He was the author of *"Studies of Hysteria, "The Dream Origin"* and *"The Development of Psychoanalysis"* to name but a few and he coined terms that that are now in everyday use. Freud cited in his *"Introductory Lectures in Psychoanalysis"* an example of unconscious forces creating slips of the tongue (Freudian slips). He related the conversation of a woman who maintained that prettiness was essential to pleasing a man. She went on to state that all a man needed was five straight limbs.

Freud stated that mental life is originally unconscious and only becomes conscious or pre-conscious (potentially conscious) in the course of a person being adapted to reality. He stated that the Ego, (our self-esteem and sense of being) grows out of the unconscious structure of an infant's mental life.

The philosopher, Gottfried Leibniz (in the 1600's), was actually the first person to introduce the idea of the unconscious which he described as perceptions which are highly obscure and confused. The fact that someone can recall having perceived something without being aware of it at the time he explained as *"little perceptions"* which come to consciousness with the benefit of hindsight; something will jolt our recollection of the event.

Freud used the name *Thanatos* to describe the Death Wish, which is a destructive impulse allowing the person to 'return to the womb' via death.

Eros is the title given to the Life Force, and the *Libido* is the Life Force expressed through the sex drive. He wrote *"Totem and Taboo"* where religion is seen as a substitute for parental authority; *"The Interpretation of Dreams"*, where he believed people dream in symbols for sexual activity because of mental censorship; and *"The Psychopathology of Everyday Life"*, stating that people's behaviour can be traced back to the experiences in the first five years of life. This is then incorporated in the unconscious mind and drives adult behaviour.

Freud became interested in the study of neurosis. He was apparently a very straight-laced man, to the extent of being almost puritanical, but believed that the conscious experience of pleasure reduces tensions produced by the libido.

Freud believed that human beings were motivated primarily by biological instincts and stated that the way these were handled by

21

the parents during vital stages in infant/child development were instrumental in shaping personality.

He believed that babies are born with the *Id*, the most powerful survival mechanism. Gratifying a child's basic instincts for food and nurturing is crucial to its survival and Freud believed that babies obtained intense physical pleasure from feeding, particularly at the breast. The *Superego* is formed by the way the parents "discipline" the infant to control the demands of the Id. In this way the *Ego* is formed. If the conflict is too intense the Ego may be damaged.

When the Ego feels threatened by punishment from the Superego, the result is moral conflict, which produces neurotic symptoms in adulthood. Defence mechanisms are erected to protect the Ego; often these justify and rationalise wrong doing in order to protect against feelings of guilt.

Freud described several stages of psychosexual development during infancy and childhood and believed that adult personality traits can be traced to fixations or conflicts encountered during these stages. Passing through these stages without trauma will produce a relatively well-balanced adult with a stable personality.

From birth to two years the infant's sensuality is focused on his mouth, both as a source of receiving nourishment and pleasurable sensations. If there are problems during this time and the infant becomes fixated at what is called the oral stage, this will affect their personality.

The *oral* personality type is emotionally intense, easily hurt, shy and retiring and often creative. They are prone to mood swings and are day-dreamers with active fantasy lives. They are often attracted, disastrously, to ruthless and shallow people. Oral personality types are prone to depression and compulsions. If deprived of oral satisfaction in their infancy they are likely to become compulsive talkers, smokers, eaters and nail biters.

During the period of pot training around two to three years, the child experiences pleasure from the passing of motions and this is known as anal eroticism. This is also the time that the child can exert power over the parents by either agreeing or refusing to pass a stool. It can be a time of immense conflict with parental authority, and the child may stool-hold as a weapon against the parents. Freud believed that trauma and conflict during this, the anal stage, would produce an adult who is prone to obsessional acts or thoughts, hypochondria and paranoia.

The *anal* personality type is mean, ruthless and shallow. The severely repressed anal personality can display intense distaste for homosexuals, but in fact could be latent homosexual themselves. These people like order, routine and discipline, are often vain, egotistical and materialistic. They are generally power seeking, brooding, jealous, suspicious and emotional vampires, kicking others when they are down, and seeking revenge for perceived injustices when the other person is at his weakest.

During the time of the *Oedipus* complex in boys and lesser so, the *Electra* complex in girls, around 4 to 5 years, the child can fear punishment (by castration) for desiring the opposite sex parent. This fear of punishment takes the form of "castration anxiety" for boys and occurs in what is known as the *Genital Stage*. Trauma leading to fixation in the Genital Stage was believed by Freud to create the hysterical adult where a person can produce all the symptoms of a serious illness but which is unconsciously intended as an attention seeking device or a method of absolving oneself from blame for self-created problems.

Male sexism could well be a product of this stage, the female child possibly being seen as inadequate because she doesn't have a penis. This idea can be reinforced when knowledge of female menstruation becomes known. The girl herself may believe that she once had a penis, which has been cut off only to leave a small stump, the clitoris, and develop what Freud called "penis envy" which can be displayed by an abnormally high need for power and control.

The *genital* personality type has little or no depth to their character. These people are generally gullible and immature. They are always showing off or acting out a part, demanding admiration. They like to be the centre of attention. They are full of compliments and promises which come to nothing. They give the impression of being frothy, witty and bright, the life and soul of the party but there is very little underneath.

Another crisis stage then comes at puberty when the sexuality formed during childhood and which is converted into affection between the ages of 5 and 12 years is re-awakened by an influx of hormones. Parental attitudes to sex in general, sex education, masturbation, homosexual experimentation and other aspects of increasing sexual maturity are important in the formation of the sexually mature adult. Adolescent sexual experiences can affect adult relationships, creating neurosis.

Carl Jung's views on how our personalities develop

Carl Jung proposed a concept of *"the Self"* which he believed to be an awareness of our unique natures and our intimate relationship with life.

The concept of human personality being divided into introvert and extravert categories was described by Carl Gustav Jung. He was a disciple of Freud who originated his own theory of the unconscious by attributing spirituality to the human condition.

He stated that introverts react to a given situation by drawing back and hesitating with an unvoiced "no" and then they respond. They feel lonely and lost in large gatherings. They are pessimistic and critical, over self-conscious and enjoy their own company. Extraverts come forward with immediate reactions to given situations confident that their behaviour is obviously right. They are keen to make relationships with the world. Their thoughts are directed towards the outside world: they dislike aloneness, think reflection morbid and tend to lack self-criticism. Extraverts tend to marry introverts and vice versa.

Jung suggested that extraverts are likely to display hysterical symptoms, whilst introverts display depressive symptoms. This is an idea that has been supported by more recent research.

Western society is extraverted particularly in the sense of material and technical development. Eastern society is introverted as regards material poverty but has greater spiritual development.

The process of civilising human beings initiated the need for a compromise between a person and society and involved the creation of a mask behind which most people live; this is called the "*persona*".

Another side to ourselves, and one which comes from the personal unconscious, (which contains our own unique set of memories) is the "*shadow*". The shadow is the inferior being in ourselves that strives for expression and comprises the darker side of our natures, the primitive impulses and negative emotions. The shadow often expresses itself in fits of uncontrolled rage.

When we dislike someone, especially if it is an unreasonable dislike, we should suspect that we actually dislike a quality of our own which we find in the other person. The shadow often appears in dreams as an inferior or very punitive person, someone with unpleasant qualities or someone we despise.

When the shadow is too strongly repressed, it acquires strength and vigour becoming dangerous and often overwhelms the personality. Often the qualities we dislike in other people are the qualities found in our own shadows.

- *A man's shadow is embodied by another man.*

- *A woman's shadow is embodied by another woman.*

The shadow is the other side to the persona and people have to find some way of living with the dark side of their nature. Good mental health depends on accepting the shadow.

Denied unconscious desires often break through because they can't be recognised; people who deny their violent feelings often kill their loved ones in a fit of rage: "crimes of passion". People who can recognise and accept their negative emotions and violent feelings can have the opportunity to change the situation that provokes them. By refusing to accept our negative emotions and repressing the shadow, we allow it to gain strength and vigour and this can overshadow the personality.

The *anima* is the unconscious female element and a male's anima comes from his mother. When a man has repressed his feminine nature, when he undervalues feminine values or treats women with neglect or contempt, it is the "dark aspect" of his personality which presents itself.

The male expression of the anima is fantasies, moods and emotional outbursts. When a man falls in love he hangs his anima, his female side, on any likely looking person.

A woman's shadow is portrayed by another woman. The animus is the unconscious male element. A female's animus comes from her father. A woman with a strong animus produces opinions and rational judgements and can crave power. The animus can provide courage and aggressiveness where necessary. Queen Boadicea and Margaret Thatcher could both be described as having a highly developed animus. The animus comes from three routes; the collective image of a man which a woman inherits; a woman's experience of masculinity which comes from contact with men, and the naturally masculine part of the personality. It is believed that Margaret Thatcher felt her father to be a very positive role model.

A well-balanced personality should be able to display both masculine and feminine aspects of behaviour.

John is a married man with a family and runs his own business as a financial consultant. In his business dealings he is shrewd and alert and insists that his clients pay his fees promptly. John likes to relax from the pressures of work by spending time with his family. He enjoys playing with his children and takes pleasure in cooking.

The expression of John's anima and animus are appropriate; his animus, the male, more aggressive side to his character is channelled into his business affairs, whilst his anima, the female side to his character, is channelled into his relationship with his children, with whom he enjoys warm and happy interactions.

Jung believed that an inherited image of a woman exists in man's unconscious mind, an *archetype*, a representation of the experience of a man with a woman since human life emerged. A man's first experience of a relationship with a woman is with his mother. It is not how the mother actually behaves that is important, but how the child interprets her behaviour. The child forms an image of women by this first experience and later this is projected onto women who are potential partners for the man. The anima is the innate capacity, described by Jung, to produce an image of a woman.

A woman possesses an inherited image of a man, which allows her to produce opinions. Her first experience of a man is with her father who will embody the animus image for the girl. As she gets older she will project this concept onto many male figures and will perceive men based on her father figure. For a woman to have a good relationship with a man, he has to conform to the assumptions that are made about him. He has to meet a need in a woman of her idea of what a man should be like, for her to enter into a relationship with him.

The anima and animus are "archetypes" of the unconscious which Jung believed are reflected in all societies and civilizations. The image of the Old Wise Man is a consistent theme of religion and everyday life, often appearing as God, Moses, the King, heroes, doctors or saviours. The Great Mother is the female counterpart of the Old Wise Man, epitomized by the Virgin Mary, the Queen, nurses and images of women who are endowed with extraordinary caring qualities, such as Florence Nightingale.

People who have a balance of both feminine and masculine traits have good emotional well-being and are able to adjust to people and events. People who score highly on masculine traits need to feel in control of their lives (this is regardless of whether the person is a man or a woman) and these people are described as being "androgynous". It does not relate to their sexuality but merely their way of functioning in the world. These people tend to have high self-esteem.

Men who grow up emotionally close to their mothers tend to have a lot of feminine traits.

Jung described four functions which help us orientate ourselves in the world and people will use their most highly developed characteristic when dealing with problems.

- *Thinking* – gives meaning and understanding.

- *Sensation* – creates perception through our senses.

- *Intuition* – tells of future possibilities and gives atmosphere which surrounds all experience.

- *Feeling* – allows us to weigh up situations and have values.

Individuation is a phenomenon, described by Jung; a spiritual journey, which he believed melted together all the different elements of the psyche, conscious and unconscious, and the person who achieves this develops an attitude that is beyond the reach of emotional entanglements and violent shocks – a consciousness detached from the world.

The psychological differences between men and women

Sex differences and their relationship to personality have been investigated. Dr Sandra Bem of Stanford University in America devised the Bem Sex Inventory which describes "masculine and feminine" traits. The feminine traits are warmth, understanding, compassion, gentleness, sensitivity to feelings, ability to express tenderness and dependency. The masculine traits are aggression, dominance, independence, competitiveness, decisiveness, ambitiousness and leadership qualities.

However, many men display "female" personality traits such as warmth and understanding, whilst women can be aggressive and dominant. It can often be the case that an ambitious, compassionate woman can display all the characteristics of both sexes, as can a sensitive but competitive man.

It has recently been discovered by Professor Colin Blakemore at Oxford University that the connections between the two hemispheres of the brain are weaker in boys than in girls. This is believed to explain why men usually attack problems using only one side of their brain, whilst women use both sides (as shown up on brain scans). This may explain why couples may experience relationship problems caused by a breakdown in communication. Women tend to approach problem solving in a different way, seeing the whole picture rather than taking the narrower view that men do. It is also believed to be an explanation for why men tend to have superiority in maths while women are better at arts related subjects.

The Inferiority Complex

Alfred Adler claimed that a sense of inferiority creates *"Will to Power"* which is a compensatory mechanism for inferiority complexes rooted in childhood.

Some of the factors which stimulate this need for power are physical deformity; the experience of being female; position in the family – the younger children generally envying the first born. Parental reaction to a child's successes and failures, whether a child is loved and accepted or neglected, hated or even spoiled contributes to feelings of inferiority.

People suffering from inferiority complexes adopt strategies for coping. When individuals successfully compensate for their sense of inferiority they strive for intellectual achievement; this is particularly the case for people who are physically handicapped. Less intellectually able people often compensate by being warm and caring. In general, successful compensation is the channelling of energy into socially useful and acceptable activities.

Overcompensation happens when people strive for unattainable goals, or perhaps by driving very large cars or living in ostentatious surroundings.

Desmond Morris has also described a lust for power being related to sexual abnormalities. Napoleon is believed to have shrivelled genitals. The results of Hitler's autopsy allegedly revealed that he had only one testicle.

Demosthenes, who became the greatest orator in Greece, had previously suffered from a stammer. He overcame his disability

by speaking with pebbles in his mouth and went on to achieve great acclaim.
People may seek to overcompensate for a sense of inferiority by holding conceited fantasies about themselves, which do not reflect their true abilities.

Adler believed that all neuroses are attempts to free oneself from feelings of inferiority in order to gain a feeling of superiority. The experience of being a child, in itself, is fundamental to creating feelings of inferiority, as children and particularly adolescents, are acutely aware of the rights in society afforded to adults which are denied to them. If they feel that they are being badly treated by over-restrictive or domineering parents, they will have a greater sense of inferiority and a greater desire for power.

A person's self-esteem is related to his or her overall adjustment. People with good self-esteem are much better "adjusted" individuals than people with low self-esteem. People with low self-esteem are more likely to have feelings of resentment, alienation and unhappiness. These people are likely to experience insomnia and psychosomatic symptoms.

People who feel good about themselves tend to be liked and in return, are tolerant of other people. People with high self-esteem attract friendships as their positive feelings about themselves are considered attractive.

People with very low self-esteem can be described as having an "inferiority" complex. The seven signs of the inferiority complex are:

- *Being sensitive to criticism*: people with inferiority complexes are aware of their weakness and shortcomings but resent it intensely when somebody else points these out. They see any form of criticism as a personal attack.

- *Having an overcritical attitude towards others*: people who do not feel good about themselves have strong negative feelings about other people. They look hard for the flaws and shortcomings of others to try to convince themselves they really aren't so bad after all.

- *Inappropriate responses to compliments*: people with very low self esteem can either be the type of person who is always fishing for compliments, or the type of person who responds to a compliment by undermining themselves.

- *Blaming others*: a person with an inferiority complex is likely to project their perceived weaknesses onto other people, which is only a short step from blaming them for their own failures.

- *Feelings of persecution*: this is an extreme version of blaming others when things go wrong, believing people are out to get you is an escape from the sense of personal responsibility for failure.

- *Avoidance of competition*: feelings of inferiority will lead to avoidance of competitive situations for fear of failure, as not coming first is clear evidence of total failure.

- *Withdrawal from socialising*: somebody with an inferiority complex will believe they are not as interesting or intelligent as others and think people perceive them that way.

The concept of people being driven for a desire for power is familiar in the field of philosophy. Frederic Nietzsche wrote in *"Also Sprach Zarathustra"* that all humans need to be powerful above all else. "Will to Power" is the ultimate reality.

"Every living being wants above everything else a higher more powerful state of being in which the manifold frustrations of his present state are overcome. It is only when man fails in his endeavour to perfect himself ....he often settles for the hunt for crude physical power over others".

Friedrich Nietzsche

Many people display very rigid personality traits which incorporate a range of behaviours which tend not to deviate from the norm and so cannot be categorised as a psychological disorder.

The *obsessive-compulsive* personality is characterised by the perfectionist who is rigid, inflexible and cannot adapt to change. These people are generally humourless, judgemental and mean, are oversensitive to criticism and are prone to be petty over trivial details.

The *paranoid* personality is generally oversensitive and suspicious and feels that people are trying to gain advantage over them. These people have a strong sense of self-importance and tend to overestimate their talents and abilities.

Individuals possessing a *schizoid* personality are very introspective people who tend to live in a fantasy world and are rather aloof and detached from others. They seem incapable of expressing affection or tenderness, lack intimate friendships and often remain unmarried. These people are often solitary intellectuals.

There is no doubt that a great deal of what is called personality is inherited. However the influence of environment cannot be ruled out. An extraverted personality living in poverty may well turn to criminality, whilst an extravert from a fairly privileged background would be more likely to become a successful entrepreneur. The stability of a person's personality can be put under intense pressure by socio-economic circumstances. Poverty and unemployment is not conducive to fostering a stable state of mind in most people.

Family dynamics are also likely to influence the personality traits people display. There are some people who "bring out the worst in us". People living in families where there is conflict can be happy with their work colleagues or friends. Introverts living with introverts can become more introverted, whilst two extraverts under the same roof may cause sparks to fly.

People do not function in a vacuum but interact with other people in their environment, which affects both the behaviour they display and the personality traits they possess.

Chapter 2
HOW WE GET ON WITH OTHER PEOPLE:
STRANGERS AND FAMILIES

"It is only shallow people who do not judge by appearances"
Oscar Wilde (1854-1900) Picture of Dorian Gray

Looking good to be treated well

When we interact with other people we often begin to communicate before we start to speak. Faces are the most effective communicators. Researchers believe that if a person's non-verbal signals contradict what they are saying, we generally believe the facial expression. The most obvious example of this would be an expression of regret by a person with a smile on their face.

Faces themselves often elicit strong stereotypes; lean and anxious faces are perceived as being associated with members of the criminal fraternity; people with round faces and rosy cheeks are usually perceived as sweet and innocent.

Physical attractiveness in itself has been shown to have certain benefits. Good looking people are treated more favourably by others and credited with more positive characteristics than unattractive people. Research has shown that attractive people are less likely to be found guilty of a crime and to be generally treated more leniently by courts.

Physically attractive people are believed to be superior to unattractive people in all respects. They are generally considered to be more confident and assertive, happier and more amiable, more perceptive and intelligent, and more exciting, humorous, flexible and friendly than their unattractive counterparts. This is known as the *"halo"* effect, where one obvious positive characteristic implies the possession of many others. Female mental patients have been noticed to be generally less attractive than average.

Looking good is deemed to be a bonus in everyday life.

Research has shown that appearance is also important in the job market and job discrimination in favour of the good-looking tends to occur. Research has suggested that attractive people are not only more likely to be chosen by employers than unattractive people but also start at a higher salary.

General appearance can also influence the way a person is treated in an emergency: a well dressed woman seen to be collapsed in the street is more likely to be helped than a woman wearing tatty clothes, who is more likely to be perceived as being drunk.

Height, in men, seems to confer status. Tall men are generally deemed to have higher status than short men, and "high status" men are usually believed to be taller than they actually are.

A person's character is also assessed from the way they are addressed by medical staff in hospitals. Research has indicated that someone admitted as an emergency, who is shabbily dressed and unshaven is less likely to be treated urgently than somebody who is more physically presentable. People smelling of alcohol, drug addicts, prostitutes, tramps, people injured in fights and suicide attempts are often judged not to need urgent medical attention. It appears that these people are considered to be less deserving than others. It may be that the best way to survive a heart attack is to look young and attractive, dress well and traditionally, disguise your deviances and keep your breath fresh.

First impressions appear to count for a lot. We tend to make a judgement of another person based on our first encounter with them, and disregard any other information about them that comes later. A person who immediately strikes us as being miserable and unfriendly will be stuck with that label even if the first impression is false.

With job interviews, it is the first ten minutes which are crucial. Employers are believed to be influenced by first impressions and if the initial stages of the interview go badly then the candidate is likely to be unsuccessful.

Making contact with other people

Eye contact is a strong and intimate channel of communication and is a regulator of intimacy in interactions. We tend not to indulge in eye contact with strangers but we do when we want to attract someone's attention (catch their eye), to show we agree or disagree with them, or to enhance our credibility. People are more likely to believe us if we look them in the eye when we tell them something. We will have eye contact with people we like.

Another non-verbal indicator is tone of voice, which is an indicator of emotions. The voice fluctuates more when emotion is displayed and remains more flat and monotone when little emotion is shown.

The amount of physical distance people choose to put between themselves and each other can be disclosing. People stand closer to people they are fond of and further away from strangers.

Intimate friends stand less than a foot and a half from each other when they are talking. Casual friends stand two and half to four feet away from each other and people in public groups like to keep a distance of about 12 feet between themselves and other strangers.

Obviously this does not apply when we are constrained by circumstance, such as in trains, buses and shopping centres.

Latin Americans, Greeks and southern Italians tend to want to stand closer to other people whilst Swedes, Scots, Germans and North Americans feel the need to have a greater than usual distance between them and other people. A meeting between, say, an Arab and a Swede, would be rather uncomfortable, with the Arab continually trying to reduce the distance between them and the Swede continually trying to increase it. Criminals convicted of violent crimes are much more sensitive to physical closeness with other people than non-violent criminals.

Researchers have studied the amount of touching that goes on between the sexes, between parents and offspring and between friends in general social situations.

Opposite sex friends touch each other the most. Girls touch their boyfriends most frequently on the head, trunk and arms, then less frequently, from the waist down. The girls' boyfriends touch them most frequently on the head, shoulders, arms and knees, and then on the trunk and leg regions, with the least touching occurring around the genitals and buttocks.

In same sex friends touching is mainly confined to the hands and arms. Males have slightly more body contact with their mothers than their fathers, mainly touching their mother's arms: mothers are more inclined to touch their son's hands.

In conversations when there is a strong bond between the listener and the speaker, the listener will mirror the postures and facial expressions of the speaker, for example smiling at the same time, or adopting the same posture such as having crossed or uncrossed legs.

The concept of personal space is an important aspect of non-verbal behaviour. Personal space refers to an area with invisible boundaries surrounding a person's body into which intruders may not come. It could be described as a buffer zone which gives protection from unknown people who could be threatening. Attempted invasion of another person's personal space by a stranger generally causes that person to move away from them and attempt to put as much distance between them as possible. A stranger entering another person's personal space creates stress and tension.

Women choose to sit closer to other women than men do to other men. This is probably a left over from our primitive origins when males were by necessity in competition with each other for females and resources.

People are generally assumed to require a large amount of personal space if they are considered to be high status. Executives of companies have their own large offices, whilst the lower status employees are often herded together in one office. High status is often conferred on people who appear to have acquired a huge amount of personal space or territory.

How body language gives us away

Body language is another word for emotional leakage. If a person is lying then they are likely to remain stiff and motionless and not talk with their hands. Hand gestures are often used unconsciously by people to illustrate and reinforce what they are saying and this is usually absent from the conversation of someone who is lying. People who are being untruthful or who are generally anxious about what they are saying tend to continually touch their faces, which indicates negative feelings about themselves. Shuffling feet during conversation often indicates anxiety. Honesty is linked with eye contact and people increase their eye contact with their conversational partners when they are eager to be seen as honest.

Someone who rubs and strokes themselves is giving themselves reassurance, whilst rubbing the arm of the chair indicates emotional restlessness. The making of a fist indicates aggression, as does the touching of one's neck and expanding one's chest.

- The touching of our noses shows that we are frightened.

- Covering our eyes with our hands indicates shame.

- Scratching or picking our faces indicates self-blame or self-attack.

- The lower lip pressed up is a sign of vulnerability.

A person who feels insecure and threatened by the situation they find themselves in will display a shoulder forward posture. They may be hunched over with the chin in a slightly crouching position. Feeling the need to get out of a situation is also displayed by the rocking of the head or the body and immobility.

When we are in the presence of people we like we will lean towards them, stand closer to them, look at them a lot, touch them and adopt a relaxed posture when speaking to them.

A face with dilated pupils is more attractive than a face with constricted pupils. A person's pupils dilate in dim light – hence low lights and soft music set the scene for romance. Having our hands in our pockets in the presence of another person is a sign of discomfort with our present circumstances. Insisting someone goes through a door before us is believed to be a power mechanism.

People who feel themselves to be in the presence of their superiors spend a lot of time looking at this person. People who like each other spend a lot of time gazing at each other when talking, even more so than people in love.

In general, however, being looked at for a long period of time creates anxiety and this is most easily tolerated by extraverts. The Japanese tend to view intensive eye contact as rude and aggressive and prefer to look at the speaker's neck when being spoken to. Arabs tend to use a lot of eye contact when conversing, whereas Western people generally alternate between eyes and mouth.

If we have mixed feelings about the person we are talking to then we are likely to have our knees pointing away and our arms crossed. Having our legs closed tightly could mean a desire to withdraw from the situation or indicate the need for self-protection.

- Touching the head is a sign of uncertainty.

- Looking down at the ground is a sign of shame or dislike.

Posture mimicry usually occurs in happily married couples and long-term friends.

Body language is much more expressive than the spoken word and facial expressions can communicate more information than we think. If there is a conflict between what a person is saying and the expression on their face, then the facial expression will be believed. A person with a deadpan expression claiming that they are 'very pleased to see you' is obviously lying and unlikely to be believed. A smile can be false or genuine: with a real smile the eyes narrow and wrinkle, whereas with a fake smile only the mouth widens and the eyes remain unchanged.

Smiling is a universal signal for happiness in most cultures throughout the world. The facial manipulations involved in smiling can create beneficial effects in the smiler as well as in the person who is being smiled at.

Blushing is a sexual signalling device in pubescent girls and often women will use blusher as part of their make-up routine in order to increase their physical attractiveness.

In threatening situations when the *fight or flight syndrome* comes into force the mouth is drawn back into a false smile, there is chewing and licking of the lips and frequent swallowing when an individual is anxious to get away from a particular situation. When the 'fight' response is elicited, the lips come apart and may be pushed forward, the chin also is pushed forward and the head may be held forward for long periods. In physical aggression the mouth is small and tight.

Conforming with other people

We prefer strangers who have similar attitudes to us and they are potential friends. The more we agree with them the more we will like them. If we find people agreeing with us when we hold unusual views, we will be strongly drawn to them. We tend to view people who look like us and think like us as being extremely attractive: the more similar someone is to us the more we will have a positive view of them.

People feel the need to conform to other people. Whether they fit in with the general prevailing norms or drop out from conventional society, they will still feel the need to belong with others and select people whose values and opinions they respect. Conformity is the way our behaviour is modified by being in the presence of others.

There are three main types of conformity:

- Group pressure forces a person to yield under the threat of rejection or the promise of a reward.

- The person pretends to conform to the values of the group to which they belong, but privately rejects their views.

- The individual selects a peer group, friends and acquaintances of the same age, beliefs, opinions, and values and adopts the set of norms they generally hold amongst them.

The researchers Asch and Sherif have both investigated people's levels of conformity where assessments of size and distance are required. The findings show that most people are reluctant to stick to their own answer if it differs from the rest of the group, even if the other members of the group are wrong. People tend to rely on the judgement of others if they are set a particularly difficult task and are more likely to accept the opinions of others when they are the only ones to have a different answer.

If the people opposing you in a decision appear to have high status, then you are more likely to concede to their judgements than if you perceive "the opposition" to be low status. You are likely to stick to your guns and stand out from the rest if you hold yourself and your opinions in high esteem and those who oppose you in low esteem. This is particularly relevant for situations such as jury service where unanimous verdicts are often required.

People who stand alone in their opinions tend to have good self-esteem, leadership qualities, high intellectual ability, good social relations, a distrust of rigid authoritarian attitudes and are assertive, lacking any sense of inferiority.

Obeying other people – a "shocking" experiment

One step removed from conformity is obedience. A famous study of obedience was carried out by Stanley Milgram at Yale University in the USA in the early 1960's. Forty men were recruited through a newspaper advertisement and were offered payment to take part in an experiment in learning. The men were greeted by Milgram in a white coat and it was explained to them that they would be teachers in a word learning task. Each man was told that if the learner made an error, he was to administer an electric shock to him by pressing a button. The shocks ranged from 15 volts (mild shock) through to "Danger: Severe Shock", and then on to 450 volts marked with XXXX which carried the assumption that this could be fatal. Each time the learner made a mistake the teacher was instructed to increase the punishment by 15 volts. The teacher witnessed the learner being strapped in a chair and a screen was then inserted between the two of them. The teacher was given a sample shock of 45 volts, to confirm the equipment was working. The learners in this situation were actually members of the research team acting the role and were not in fact connected to the electrical equipment.

People who were interviewed about this experiment and asked to predict the teacher's behaviour, believed that very few people would actually administer the severe electric shocks. Psychiatrists claimed that only sadists and psychopaths would keep shocking the learners to the maximum voltage and that most would stop at fairly low levels.

Throughout the course of this experiment Stanley Milgram took on the role of the white-coated supervisor and urged reluctant teachers to carry on with the shocks thus creating the crucial factor in the experiment - pressure from an authority figure. The "teaching" began at 75 volts and the learner cried out in pain, demanding to be released because he suffered from a heart condition.

At "Severe Shock" he twitched and screamed with pain. At even higher voltages there was silence; the teachers were told to treat this lack of response as an incorrect answer and increase the shock.

During this exercise the "teachers" suffered fits of nervous laughter sweated and groaned, trembled and dug their fingernails into their skin, but still carried on shocking. Some 62% of the teachers obeyed the supervisor and shocked their "learners" to the 450 volts 'fatal' level. Everyone in the study continued to give shocks to the 300 volts – fairly severe shock level, at which level the learners would pound with their fists and scream in agony.

In a modification of this experiment where the teachers and learners sat side by side instead of separated from view by a screen, lower levels of obedience were found, as the teachers found it more difficult to cause suffering when they could witness their victim's plight.

The results of this study of obedience showed that these men were very obedient to authority and were apparently prepared to cause severe suffering, and even possibly commit murder when responsibility was accepted by an authority figure giving orders. When this experiment was replicated in Germany 85% of the teachers were fully obedient to the supervisor. However, it is not known whether this experiment was carried out in other countries.

The implications of Milgram's work are disturbing, showing that people are prepared commit acts of appalling cruelty when personal responsibility for their actions is sanctioned by authority. Only men were used as subjects.

Blind obedience to authority could, in fact, be a facet of the hierarchical organisation of human society in which individuals are required to function within the system. A feature of this is authoritarian child-rearing methods, the child being forced into blind obedience to its parents for fear of punishment and thus creating the *"Authoritarian personality"*. Such a system of childrearing was common practice in Germany in the years leading up to the rise of Hitler, who was reared by a brutal father. The underlying criteria for the creation of the Authoritarian personality are believed to be the over-control of emotions, combined with the denial of anger towards the parents during childhood and the displacement of this anger onto other groups during adulthood.

Helping strangers

Studies have been made of the human capacity to help strangers in trouble. If we are so willing to punish other people, will this affect our capacity to offer assistance in times of crisis?

Prompted by the case of a woman called Kitty Genovese who was stabbed to death in full view of passers-by in New York State some years ago, the researchers Latané and Darley investigated the phenomenon of "bystander apathy". The bulk of this research concentrates on what has been observed in real life situations, that is, the more people present at an accident or witnessing somebody collapsed in the street, the less likely it is that the person will be helped. This creates a diffusion of responsibility, where each person present at the scene of the crisis tends to assume that somebody else in the group will take the responsibility for helping.

If it is a road accident, each new passer-by who congregates at the scene will assume that the people gathered there would have carried out first aid and sent for an ambulance. If it is somebody collapsed on a pavement the attitude of the people already congregated is also important. If each new passer-by arriving is met with the attitude "I think they are drunk" then this will set the scenario for each new person arriving on the scene.

In situations of women being assaulted in public whom people believed to be the wives or girlfriends of the man attacking them, passers-by are unlikely to get involved, as they tend to place some responsibility on the woman for having provoked the attack.

In staged violent situations involving couples in public, only 19% of passers-by were prepared to intervene when they assumed the struggle to be the result of a personal dispute.

Some 65% of passers-by were prepared to intervene if they thought someone was being attacked by a stranger.

The effects of having power

The possession of power can be a crucial factor in affecting the way people behave towards each other.

Phillip Zimbardo investigated the dehumanisation that is so prevalent in prisons. His idea was that ordinary members of society would be persuaded to act as guards and prisoners in a mock-up of a real prison, where the environment that inmates experience would be replicated exactly. He wanted to observe the effects of ordinary people having power, and being on the receiving end of it, by creating the unpleasant conditions that are found in real prisons. He was trying to discover whether it is the personalities of the prisoners and guards that make prison life so appalling or the situation of being contained in prison itself.

A number of college students volunteered to take part in this research project, known as the Stanford Prison Experiment, and agreed for it to be as close to real life as possible. A quiet Sunday morning in April 1971 was disrupted by a screeching squad car siren as police swept through the Palo Alto city streets picking up the volunteer prisoners for a surprise mass arrest. Other prisoners and guards were recruited through newspaper advertisements. The volunteers were all male, and mainly middle-class students. They were tested to make sure they were intelligent, mature and had very few anti-social tendencies. The volunteers were selected at random to be either prisoners or guards.

All of the suspects were charged with a crime, read their rights, spread-eagled against the police car, searched, handcuffed and taken away in the back seat of the police car to the police station. The whole operation was carried out realistically with the co-operation of the police department. The suspects were charged and taken to "Stanford County Prison" which was, in reality the basement laboratories of Stanford University converted into a mock prison. The volunteer prisoners were then stripped naked, deloused, and issued with a uniform, bedding and basic supplies. The uniform consisted of a loose fitting muslin smock, no underclothes, a light chain and lock around one ankle, rubber sandals and a cap made from a nylon stocking. This clothing effectively degraded the volunteer prisoners in the eyes of their guards.

The "*power game*" then came into play. The volunteer guards told the volunteer prisoners that there were sixteen rules of prisoner conduct, starting with the rule that prisoners must address the guards as "Mr Correctional Officer" and finishing with the rule that failure to obey the rules would result in punishment. The guards were required, for the purposes of the experiment, to keep the necessary order for the prison to function effectively but were prohibited from using physical aggression. The guards wore a uniform consisting of plain khaki shirts and trousers, a police stick and reflecting sunglasses. This, therefore, would have created anonymity in the guards, particularly allowing them to avoid eye contact with their prisoners.

Although most of the participants in this experiment were educated middle-class men and had willingly volunteered to help in this psychological research, within two days violence and rebellion had broken out.

The prisoners ripped off their clothing, shouted and cursed at the guards and barricaded themselves inside their cells. The guards put down the rebellion violently, using fire extinguishers and then systematically harassed their prisoners. One of the volunteer prisoners showed such severe symptoms of emotional disturbance in the form of uncontrollable crying and screaming that he had to be released.

On day three of the experiment a rumour spread through the prison about a mass escape plot and Philip Zimbardo, who had taken on the role of "Prison Superintendent" instructed the guards to take very repressive action against the prisoners. Increasingly the men recruited to take the role of the guards appeared to be deriving a great deal of satisfaction from exercising power and behaving in a sadistic manner. Force and aggression by the guards increased steadily from day to day in spite of the fact that prisoner resistance declined and evaporated. About one third of the guards were so consistently hostile and degrading to their prisoners that they could be described as sadists.

Zimbardo's fiancée visited the experimental prison and on seeing a line of blindfolded prisoners shuffling under guard to the toilets demanded that the experiment should be ended immediately.

What happened in this mock prison was so unpleasant and potentially dangerous that the entire experiment was brought to an end after only one week instead of the intended two.

It appears from this study that environmental situations can often create conditions which bring out the worst in human nature. It is often said that power tends to corrupt and absolute power corrupts absolutely. This could be borne out by a statement made before the experiment by one of the volunteer guards. He wrote that he was a pacifist and was so unaggressive that he couldn't imagine ill-treating another human being, yet by day three of his role as prison guard he appeared to be thoroughly enjoying manipulating people. He later remarked that he really enjoyed having almost total control over everything that was said and done.

Attitudes are normally maintained and often re-evaluated by interacting with other people, listening to their opinions and watching their behaviour. If social or political trends create a majority with different attitudes to us, we can find ourselves feeling uncomfortably isolated and either change our attitudes to fit in with the general way of thinking or seek out other people who share our own belief systems and "frame of reference".

Our attitudes towards other people and our relationships with them are a means to meet and master the world.

Threats to our state of being often occur when what is apparent in the outside world contradicts what we think, feel and believe. This is called cognitive dissonance and we are forced to rethink our beliefs and ideas in order to reduce internal psychological conflict. Retaining a stable psychological state is known as cognitive consonance.

A researcher called Festinger described this phenomenon when he went undercover with a religious sect who had predicted the end of the world by a large tidal wave on a certain date, and he camped with them half-way up a mountain at the appointed time. The tidal wave failed to materialise, which obviously produced a great deal of cognitive dissonance amongst the cult members. Their strategy for reducing this conflict was to claim that "God had changed his mind". Festinger decided that there must be a balance between items of information, beliefs, values and attitudes to avoid psychological tension and to maintain cognitive consonance and credibility with other people.

There is evidence to show that although we possess different attitudes about other people, situations and events, research has shown that people have a tendency to say one thing and do another. American motel owners claimed that they would refuse to serve Chinese people in their restaurants, but Chinese researchers who attempted to eat in these very same restaurants were treated courteously treated by the owners.

Families

"All happy families resemble one another, but each unhappy family is unhappy in its own way"
Leo Tolstoy (1828-1910) Anna Karenina

Most people establish a strong enough pair bond to want to enter into marriage or a long-term partnership and although it is generally considered a private agreement between two consenting adults, very many other factors come into play. Parents and other family members can attempt to influence a person's choice of partner, as this person will be absorbed into the respective family units of each individual entering into the relationship. The reasons for entering into the marriage or co-habitation are very important, often it is just to gain independence from parents that people get married or they feel unable to live alone either for social, psychological or financial reasons.

Living with a loved one involves re-establishing an individual's relationship with their family. Their roles of daughter or son become diminished as their role of husband/wife becomes established.

Families are the major social settings in which we learn about ourselves, others and relationships.

When the children are born the family dynamics change significantly as in-laws become grandparents and husband/wives become mothers/fathers and this can be a time of crisis within a family unit.

Although marriage brings into with it a certain degree of behaviour that has been influenced by the partner's own experience of growing up in a family and witnessing the strengths and weaknesses of their own parent's marriage, parenthood can bring many conflicts with regard to marital relationships.

In the absence of any clear cut independent ideas or sound advice in this respect, couples often fall back on their own parents' strategies of child rearing, bringing their children up in the same way that they were raised.

The child itself can create a love triangle and most often it is the father who feels rejected and his partner invariably becomes totally involved with her child. The child can also become a scapegoat for its parent's problems which existed before it was born but remain unresolved and flare-up again with the child acting as a catalyst.   Children often become the focus of the parents' conversation, they being unable to communicate directly as a couple.

A closer look at this family situation may reveal that a woman may feel her husband to be a bad father and her children would be less demanding of her attentions if he were to take a more active role in the family. She blames him to a certain extent for her psychological state. He refuses to acknowledge that her feelings and behaviour are in any way related to his shortcomings and considers her to be a bad mother because she can't cope. His behaviour then reinforces his wife's beliefs about him; her behaviour reinforces her husband's beliefs about her and the children respond negatively to being caught up in the atmosphere of stress and tension. One party may side with the child against the other party, thus denigrating their value as a mother/father and calling into question that parent's femininity/masculinity. In the case of single parents, the grandmother often steps in to enter into a dispute with the mother or the father over the child's upbringing, creating another dimension to the problem.

In most societies, the transition from one stage to another is marked by some type of ceremony or ritual. Family therapists often create rituals in order to help families deal with such situations as bereavement and divorce where the feelings surrounding these events remain unresolved. It is believed that the decline of ceremonies and rituals and greater freedom from formalities, has produced greater confusion about the position of children, parents, grandparents, etc.

In primitive societies puberty particularly is subject to a ritual and the pubescent boy has a clear sense of moving from boyhood to manhood. In the case of girls nature often performs this function with the onset of menstruation which is a definite dividing line between being a girl and a woman. Although boys develop male adult bodily features, this is a gradual transition.

Childbirth and dealing with the young is a major stage in family life and a time when the previous pattern of life of the partners may become disrupted. During the period of middle marriage the children are established at school and the pattern of family life has time to stabilise. Children leaving home create new pressures, as the partners in the relationship now have to negotiate their pattern of living. The woman finds that her children, having been a major focus of her attention for very many years, are now gone and she again looks at her husband as a life partner to meet her needs and may find him lacking.

Looking at malfunctioning families

The interactions between family members have been the subject of research. The members of a family influence each other and are influenced by each other. Individuals create a family unit. Central to the notion of functioning is cause and effect. If a woman is depressed and irritable, this will inevitably affect her relationship with her husband and her children. Her husband may then psychologically withdraw from her, the children react by misbehaving and their father may then respond to the bad behaviour with aggression, causing his wife to become even more depressed.

Milton Erickson was one pioneer of "family therapy", work which was carried on by Jay Haley and which identified the various crises that people experience during different stages of their lives, both as individuals and within the family group. He reported that unhappy families have habitual styles of poor interactions. They get caught in a pattern of arguments.

Internal distress and unhappy feelings become expressed in ritualised behaviour. The family members' behaviour patterns do not fit well: one person may talk about one topic and another replies by talking about something completely different.

Distressed families have high rates of monologue – silence, in that one person does all the talking while the other person remains silent, whether it be listening or shutting off completely.

Malfunctioning families do not support each other and show little affection to each other. They display rigid and predictable behaviour patterns.

During childhood and up until independence, young people are dependent upon their parents for shelter, food and financial support and are to greater or lesser extent obliged to abide by their parents' wishes in order to obtain these things. At adolescence there comes a need to break free from the family unit, establish independence and form sexual relationships in order to produce their own offspring.

In the animal kingdom the transition from dependant child to sexually active adult is fairly straightforward. Mother bears have been seen to abandon their offspring at an appropriate time in their development. The parents play no role in the selection of a mate or the rearing of their offspring's young; therefore the mother bear does not become a mother-in-law or grandmother in the human sense of the term and does not have the complication of being involved in an extended family.

As children become adults they lose the previous tolerance they experienced and they are expected to adopt adult responsibilities. This relates to separating themselves from the family unit both physically and psychologically and establishing an independent living area. Many people fail to achieve this level of maturity and in the animal kingdom are known as peripherals. These are males who have failed to establish a territory and who are therefore sexually rejected by females, and females who have not been selected as mates by males are treated as outcasts by females with status i.e. those with sexual partners.

In malfunctioning families the capacity for change is essential. Often a couple may indulge in "meta-arguments" - that is arguments about arguments without actually getting to the root of the problem. A husband and wife fighting violently, even to the point of causing injury could be making a dramatic attempt to get closer to each other.

A tyrannical husband may create an apathetic wife. He may say "she can never do anything without my telling her", to which she is likely to reply "he is always bullying me and making all the decisions so it is pointless for me to do anything".

One partner's alcoholism or sickness may be reinforced by the other partner as a method of control. If the partner attempts to overcome the illness or alcoholism, then the stability of the partnership is under threat; the other partner in the relationship may not be able to cope with someone sober or healthy who may demand gratification of his or her needs.

The value of the traditional nuclear family has been disputed for many years. The Psychiatrist R.D. Laing saw the family as a potential breeding ground for neuroticism and psychosis. Feminists have long believed that mothers are naturally the best parents for children. They claim that fatherhood is a socially constructed role, which most men fail to successfully achieve, creating considerable problems in the process. However, Desmond Morris describes forms of social aggression by the naked ape which includes the territorial defence of the family unit within the larger group and the personal and individual maintenance of hierarchy positions.

Children from two-parent families have fewer cases of delinquency and failure at school than children from one parent families. The Report report *"Crime and the Family"*, carried out in 1993, studied one thousand children and found that seven out of ten children lacking poor parental care before the age of five became delinquent. Shared family activities were also seen as good indicators of better adjusted children. The report identifies poor parental supervision; harsh, neglectful or erratic discipline and parental strife as potential causes of teenage delinquency.

Very often children resemble their grandparents and deep-rooted emotional and unresolved conflicts which have lain dormant since their own childhood can often arise between parent and child. When a child displays undesirable aspects of a grandparent's personality, then problems can arise.

Daniel possesses very many personality traits of his grandfather. He is very argumentative and refuses to see his mother's point of view. He is tall and has a very deep voice for a boy of his age and when engaged in a dispute with his mother, often uses his height and booming voice as a weapon with which to intimidate her.

Susan, when engaged in a conflict with her son, is reminded of her dealings with her father when she was younger. Daniel has a similar temperament and her father used to use his superior height and deeper voice to intimidate her during an argument. When she has confrontations with her son, much of the unresolved anger she felt as a teenager towards her father rears up and she can often become very distressed during these arguments with her son.

Family life became a focal point for research into mental illness in the 1960's. R.D. Laing maintained that a deviant person was often the only normal member of an abnormal family and failure to comply with their wishes created a situation where they were labelled by the other family members as either mad or bad.

Abnormal communication patterns can have a very destructive influence on the mental health of family members.

Gavin's mother has always found it difficult to communicate directly with people and her way of expressing anger and dissatisfaction with family members is to ignore them in some type of "game playing" scenario where they have to guess what they have done to upset her. Gavin finds this profoundly disturbing as it is difficult for him to know what he has to do to rectify it. His mother also has a tendency to tell other family members and friends about anything her son may have done to upset and offend, often within earshot of him, and this creates a very strong sense of paranoia. Gavin then starts believing that every time there is a conversation within the family it is about him and he tries to eaves-drop on his mother's telephone conversations thinking they are always negatively related to him.

In his own personal life, Gavin has found that he is also unable to communicate effectively with his partner and his friends and resorts to talking in riddles, sarcasm and snide remarks if he disagrees with someone else's point of view. Gavin's mental health is often borderline, with him living his life feeling paranoid and adopting his mother's trait of talking about people in a disapproving way when they are in earshot.

Being the "black sheep" of the family has been associated with general deviance such as drug taking, alcoholism and petty crime.

59

In a larger context a "deviant" member of a family, for example a wayward son or daughter can effectively remove the onus from the parents to discuss and solve their own problems. They are likely to focus their attention on the disruptive teenager as a cause of their arguments. In reality the teenager's behaviour may be the result of parental disharmony and the disruptive behaviour an attempt to draw attention to the unhappiness this is causing. The cycle may repeat itself until it either becomes resolved by the teenager leaving home or the parents divorcing.

In the nuclear family a "power pattern" has usually been established between the sexual partners early in the relationship, with one partner being dominant and the other submissive. In destructive family environments the dominant parent may try to force his or her personality on to other members of the family. If the person wielding the power is extraverted they may accuse the more introverted members of the family of being sullen and uncommunicative. If on the other hand that person is introverted they may perceive the extraverted members of the family as being silly and frivolous. The inability to understand each other's moods within a family setting can lead to conflict and tension.

As the children grow into adults they strive to be as powerful as their parents and this can lead to intense conflict and threaten the stability of an already established framework of interacting.

If, within the family environment, there is conflict between a "dominant" father and his son, a usually submissive and passive mother may intervene to reduce the conflict. This will then increase the tension between her and her husband as she is stepping out of her usual role to challenge his power. From the father's viewpoint his authority is being challenged from two directions from previously passive sources; firstly a submissive wife and secondly a son that could previously be controlled.

A passive and submissive father with daughters can often feel threatened if he perceives that the women in the family, who outnumber him, are overpowering beyond what he feels is acceptable to his masculinity.

Dysfunctional families often use one member as a scapegoat and form coalitions against this one person. In a family with grown up children a father may be targeted as the focal point for all that is wrong. Often this is cultivated by the mother from an early age and because of her discontent with her husband's failings she may deliberately foster in her young children a negative concept of their father which stays with them all of their lives. This is done to ensure their loyalty to her but can also affect their adult personal relationships in later life.

Tense family situations may also be complicated by racial factors.

Donald was put into care at the age of 10 because as a single parent his mother was unable to cope with his disruptive behaviour, which included petty crime. He leaves the children's home at the age of 16 and finds lodgings away from the town in which he is brought up in. At 19 he emigrates to South Africa during the apartheid years, and unconsciously absorbs a lot of the prevailing culture. At the age of 45 with a family of his own, he tracks down his mother and on being reunited with her discovers that she has married an Afro-Caribbean man and has had four children by him. He returns to South Africa with an overwhelming sense of rejection, which is reinforced by the fact that his mother not only has a new family, but it is on an interracial level, a concept alien to him, deeply ingrained by the culture in which he lived for many years.

Tanya was the child of an interracial marriage, her mother being white and her father being black. Her mother leaves when she is only a few months old and her father hands her over to his mother. His own mother, now with a new partner has just given birth herself and feeds both her own new son and her granddaughter at her breast. Tanya grows up in a household where she is of mixed race, the rest of the family is black, and she has a brother/sister relationship with a boy the same age, who is actually her uncle.

It could be argued that it is a very damaging situation when a father promotes the idea in his children's minds that they have a bad mother. This is likely to occur when marriage difficulties arise and the husband seeks revenge against his wife by alienating the children from her.

Of all the interactions people go through it is probate which could be described as the most complex as these involve the most intense emotions.

Investment in one's genes is arguably the most important investment that a person will ever make.

Chapter 3
OUR LOVES, OUR MARRIAGES AND OUR DIVORCES

Love

"Come live with me, and be my love, And we will all the pleasures prove..."
                                    Christopher Marlowe 1564-1593

Kinds of Loving

Over the centuries there have been attempts to explain the feeling that we call love. "Eros", the God of Love, was described by an ancient Greek philosopher as the God "who loosens the limbs and damages the mind".

More recently Psychologists have taken an analytical perspective on this very strong emotion.

A researcher, called Lee, in *"The Colors of Love"* described six types of love.

*Romantic love (**Eros**)* is sensual and physical. It focuses on such phenomena as love at first sight and emphasises the importance of beauty and physical perfection. The attraction in this type of love is sexual and the bonding of partners is mainly an intense physical attraction.

*Game playing love (**Ludus**)* is a more frivolous type of love where the lover sees a relationship in terms of game playing, flirtation and having fun. The emphasis in this type of love is the lack of commitment, the enjoyment coming from teasing and playfulness. People who display this type of loving strategy will often end a

63

relationship when it stops being fun and deliberately choose partners to whom they know they will feel little commitment.

Friendship love (**Storge**) is dispassionate and based on the sharing of similar interests and enjoyment of mutual activities. Excitement and physical sensuousness do not play an important role for people who display this type of love in interpersonal relationships.

Possessive/dependent love (**Mania**) is uncertain, anxious, obsessive and possessive. These lovers are very jealous and are the type of people who attempt suicide to regain their partner's attention. The emphasis is on possessing their partner's body and soul and this actually seems to destroy the relationship.

Shopping list love (**Pragma**) is characterised by the perceived strengths and weaknesses of the partners who consciously consider their prospective partner's background, attitudes, religion, politics, hobbies etc, before committing themselves to a relationship. The people who display this type of "love strategy" are unromantic and level headed.

All-giving selfless love (**Agape**) is compassionate and unconditional. It is felt and given despite the behaviour of the loved one. This resembles the type of love that a mother feels for her children and is the type of love in adult relationships where one of the partners gains strength by having a weaker person dependent upon them.

According to research, men are Erotic and Ludic in their loving strategies but women tend to be Pragmatic, Manic and Storgic when it comes to having an emotional relationship.

People may display a mixture of these strategies during the course of the relationship and it is fairly safe to assume that people fall into one of these categories; their personal loving strategy dictates their choice of long-term partner and may well be the factor which determines whether the relationship succeeds or fails.

Women tend to have the desire to fall in love and look for relationships where they can be in love. Men tend to look for someone to love.

Often partners in relationships bear a strong physical resemblance to each other, almost as if that person were looking at their partner and seeking his or her own opposite-sex mirror image reflected back at them.

Although different types of loving have been described it is difficult to offer one particular explanation for what attracts one person so strongly to another. We know that "one man's meat is another man's poison", that "opposites attract", and that many people often speak of their partners as "my other half" or "my better half". This implies a basic instinct for pair bonding at sexual maturity which is believed to be a biological programme to ensure the survival of the human race.

We know that "two heads are better than one" and in successful partnerships there is a blending of skills, characteristics and temperaments which allow a couple to function as one multi-faceted individual when the circumstances dictate.

A Staircase to Heaven

The concept of romantic love has been studied and appears to have three stages. This is known as the *"Rubin Love Scale"*.

Stage One

This is the stage of giddy happiness, elation and a "love rush" which has a duration of two and a half years. This phenomenon appears to be biological in origin, as it is long enough for a human being to conceive, give birth and give the infant parental nurturing in its early years.

Couples in love have undergone brain scans and a large amount of the "pleasure" brain chemical dopamine has been found in the pleasure centres of the brain. Couples in love can experience sensations similar to those produced by cocaine, and there is an increased focussing on the loved one as the source of pleasure.

Stage Two

Couples in this stage of love want to spend a lot of time together. People who are "obsessively" in love show symptoms similar to *"Obsessive-Compulsive Personality Disorder"*, and display reduced amounts of the brain chemical serotonin, which is usually associated with depression.

Stage Three

This stage of love produces calmer behaviour but still creates the need for the couple to have contact with each other and a long term need to touch each other.

People often talk of a certain chemistry between them, or a magnetic attraction, and it may well be that by forming relationships, people are responding to body chemistry by intellectualising what their bodies are telling them to do. In other words after having been physically attracted to another persons chemistry, positive characteristics of that person are created to explain what they are feeling e.g. she is beautiful (often she isn't), he is intelligent (often he isn't) and to block out the negative characteristics – "love is blind". As the song goes "I don't know why I love you, but I do".

Women and men differ markedly in their loving strategies and general behaviour, hence the fact that "the course of true love never runs smoothly".

Sex differences are evident in behaviour during love affairs, in that a man is likely to fall in love with a woman at an earlier point in the relationship. A woman takes longer to be sure of her feelings. Men tend to hang on after the relationship has deteriorated. Women fall in love later in a relationship and will seek to end it when it is obviously failing. It is a woman who is more likely to end the relationship than a man.

Men tend to fall in love on the basis of female physical attractiveness and the anticipated pleasure and fun that the relationship would bring. Women are believed to take a more practical approach to potential relationships, not relying so heavily on the physical aspects and possibility of fun-filled romance that their partner may bring, but wanting also the back up of good character, attitudes and financial solvency.

This seems plausible considering that courtship occurs during the fertile years when a woman will be instinctively driven to seek out a suitable father for her offspring, whist a male is biologically driven to seek out opportunities to fertilise a female and pass on his genes.

Men in fact are more romantic than women and very many women appear to be happy to marry a man they don't love if he is acceptable in every other way.

In discussing love it is important to distinguish between loving someone, liking someone, being fond of someone and being in love with someone.

It is believed that the first love is the strongest and all other love affairs after this are weaker and less successful. This seems to be borne out by the fact that second marriages have less chance of surviving than first marriages – although this could be for other reasons, such as taking on stepchildren or financial problems caused by supporting the children from a previous relationship.

It could be argued that love is an intense sexual attraction which is then modified into a mental framework of perceived pleasures, with the positive attributes of that person created in the lover's mind.

High on the list of requirements for a life partner must obviously be friendship, honesty, love and trust, as without these there can obviously be no strong foundations for a good relationship. Also the qualities of needing, caring and tolerance would be considered necessary.

Liking is very different to loving. Respect for a person seems to be central to liking and is not necessarily a component of loving. Many people appear to be in love with somebody they don't like or respect but this may be just an intense physical attraction that is hard to break. Early emotional experience plays an important role in a person's capacity to give and receive love. It is likely that people love others who display the qualities that their parents lacked, thus transferring their infantile love to another adult who can provide what they missed out on in infancy. They may also love a partner who possesses qualities they desire for themselves, but lack. In fact a complementary personality who makes them feel complete.

The Green-Eyed Monster

As there are different varieties of love, so there are different varieties of jealousy (as identified by a Psychologist called Mazur).

The *possessively jealous* person tends to treat their partner as though they were a personal possession. Jealousy can be felt when one partner insists on having their own independent life as well as a life with their partner, and particularly if this involves hobbies, work and other activities which involve a lot of contact with the opposite sex.

The *fearfully jealous* person generally has feelings of loneliness and rejection and dislikes being left alone by their loved one.

Competitive jealousy arises when a person is in direct competition with their partner, who may possess skills and talents that they lack. They may become jealous and resentful of the partner's achievements and success.

Having fixed and rigid views that we are right and a partner is always wrong is called *egotistical jealousy* and conflicts occur when one partner insists on holding a different viewpoint and expressing it in his behaviour.

Exclusive jealousy arises when we feel excluded from our partner's life and cannot accept that he or she has a right to activities that do not involve us.

Men tend to feel jealous when they feel inadequate and this tends to take the form of anger. This is often taken to its absolute extreme when one of the partners in a marriage, often the husband, commits murder. It is a recurring scenario that men murder their wives and children and then take their own lives after the breakdown of marriage. *"Jilted husband murders family"* is a frequent headline in newspapers.

Why do men behave like this? Often husbands believe their wives to be their property. Possibly the financial cost of a divorce is enough to "tip them over the edge".

"A crazed businessman is on the run a week after he locked his wife in a toilet and drove at it with a JCB. It is believed the incident was sparked by a dispute over a divorce settlement..."

"She was in a desperate state .... And saying her husband was trying to kill her".

Women feel jealous when the stability of what they see is a good relationship is threatened and there is no alternative relationship to go to: they react to this jealousy by becoming depressed.

If we feel that we are putting more effort into a relationship than our partner then we will feel angry and resentful. A relationship must offer a sense of fairness for it to be attractive and for us to want to stay in it. On the other hand if we perceive our partner putting more into the relationship than we are, then we may feel guilty.

The most intimate and enduring personal relationships are based on a sense of equality: the rewards and costs of keeping it going. People tend to calculate profits on the basis of cost/benefit analysis and seek to maximise them with the intention of securing the best outcome for themselves. It appears they apply market forces to their intimate lives. Considerations of equity can be very influential in determining the viability and pleasantness of a relationship.

Marriage

"Married couples who love each other tell each other a thousand things without talking"
Chinese proverb

The average courtship period before marriage is believed to be 18 months to 2 years, but there are different types of courtship which lead towards marriage and which have been described by Psychologists.

"Accelerated-arrested" courtship begins with a high level of confidence that the relationship will lead to marriage but slows down in its final progression to marital commitment.

Brian & Alison are instantly attracted. They both feel they have met the right person for them and enjoy some mutual activities and can function as partners. They also have separate friends and hobbies. As the day of their marriage draws near they start to get cold feet. Are they certain about the commitment? Will being married change their relationship? Brian has friends that Alison doesn't like and vice versa. Will that affect their married life?

"Accelerated" courtship starts off more slowly than Brian and Alison's courtship but proceeds more smoothly to the certainty of eventual marriage.

Lorraine and Adam like each other a great deal but go more tentatively into the relationship. They take things slowly and cautiously but their courtship runs smoothly and eventually they

71

get married. There are very many things they don't have in common.

"*Intermediate*" courtship again goes along slowly and gradually but in the run up to the marriage a lot of conflict arises in the last stages.

Theresa and Anthony have a good relationship which involves a good quality physical relationship and enjoyment of shared interests but they are both very independent people and insist on "doing their own thing" separately which means they spend a lot of time away from each other.

"*Prolonged*" courtships develop slowly and uncertainly with much turbulence and difficulty.

Christine and Dominic have an instant sexual attraction but both have very strong personalities which often clash but in different ways. Their relationship is very much a power struggle. Dominic tends to engage in "emotional power games" and "passive aggression" whereby if it is Christine's birthday and she has said something to upset him he will deliberately "forget" to buy a card and present, claiming not to know it was her birthday. Christine in turn takes revenge on Dominic, who finds difficulty in coping with confrontation, by stating very forcefully how dissatisfied she is with his behaviour.

Although eventually they get married the patterns of behaviour persist in the marriage creating intense disharmony.

Marital harmony – give and take

Attraction to the idea of being married to a certain person is believed to result from each partner sensing in the other person that they will fulfil a deeply held need. This causes the marriage to be in a state of "push-pull" where one marriage partner has the conflict between being intimate with their husband/wife, but also pulling back in order to preserve their own identity and not being "swallowed up" by the other person. In order to achieve "distance" people often start an argument just in order to obtain some personal space from their partners. Often the "making up" after emotional conflict achieves a better level of intimacy.

Communication is a key factor in a successful marriage. Research carried out into the happiness of married couples has shown that happily married couples give more positive non-verbal cues (such as touching, smiling, etc) than unhappily married couples. Satisfied couples support each other both verbally and practically.

Happy couples tend to approve of each others ideas and suggestions. They try harder to avoid having rows and arguments. They are more willing to reach compromises on difficult decisions and are generally more affectionate towards each other. Happy couples agree with each other.

Couples will feel happy together if they are fairly closely matched for physical attractiveness, intelligence, and sociability. If they feel that they love each other equally and are committed to each other, if they fit in well with each other's families and friends and have joint access to the finances, then their relationship will be harmonious. Failure to achieve equity in these areas, and the feeling that one has fewer choices and freedoms in one's life than one's partner, will create dissatisfaction and dissent.

Compatibility is not necessarily the most important ingredient. How you deal with differences is more important than feeling you are compatible. Negotiated compromise is the key element in a happy marriage. It could be argued that the best person to discuss one's marriage problems with is one's husband/wife.

It is not always necessary that the equity should take the form of similar qualities. An attractive woman can marry an unattractive but rich man – he gets beauty, she gets money – the rewards, in their eyes may be evenly balanced. This is known as a trade-off where on a psychological level partners barter their personal assets in the market place of love. When one partner constantly feels he or she is getting raw deal they will end the relationship.

The ability to adapt to marriage is largely dependent on the individual and the type of person he or she is.

"Traditional" people tend to hold conventional views about marriage and family life, dislike change and intertwine their lives with their marriage partner. They are prepared to confront conflicts but only in a limited way.

"Independent" people tend to hold rather less conventional views about marriage and family life: they confront conflicts, liking to be frank and open and enjoy exploring novelty and change in their marriage.

"Separate" people are not particularly persuaded about the desirability of marriage and family life, tend not to talk intimately with their partners. These people like their own personal space, are emotionally distant from their husbands and wives and will avoid conflict with them.

Although it is commonly believed that it is women who desire the married state, it is actually men who benefit from being married. Married men are less likely to commit suicide and are generally healthier than unmarried men. Single men tend to have more problems with drink and drug abuse than married men.

Men who are widowers or divorcees suffer high rates of sudden death and severe health difficulties.

However, the picture is significantly different for women; with single women reporting generally being happier and healthier. There is a gradual decrease in happiness over the first 10 years of marriage but it increases after the children leave home.

Marital disharmony – tug of war

There are hierarchies in marriage where one partner is dominant and the other is submissive. One can be nurturant (the caretaker) and the other can be the succorant (the one taken care of). People tend towards complementary relationships where the giver is received, where a partner's good judgement is respected by a loved one who doubts his own judgement and where the organiser lives with someone who enjoys being organised.

If this balance is disrupted by life events and unforeseeable circumstances, then it can lead to tremendous conflicts.

Alan and Carol have been married for several years and the relationship has worked out very well. Alan is a pleasant methodical man, a bit of a plodder who goes to work, watches T.V, plays a bit of golf and participates in things which Carol has organised for the family. Carol enjoys being the active partner and takes responsibility for all the decisions regarding the family.

A crisis has occurred because Carol has contracted M.E. (Myalgic Encephalomyelitis) so she is sick, with a lowered resistance to infection, and apart from the loss of energy and physical illness – permanently suffering from severe flu symptoms – her self-perception of being active, organised and in control has been deeply affected. Now both the running of the domestic side of

75

family life and the major financial decisions are left to Alan, who being a naturally passive person, finds difficulty in coping. He has little experience of dealing with the things Carol previously dealt with and family life starts to fall apart. The stress of perceiving Alan as being unable to cope, particularly with the children and their problems exacerbates Carol's illness, which in turn panics Alan even more.

The previously well-balanced roles are now reversed. Alan is forced into the active role which he finds uncomfortable and Carol is placed in the passive roles which causes her distress.

People who marry young, people with psychiatric problems and unequal matching for age, race and religion are more likely to divorce. The more sexual partners a person has before marriage, or settling down, the more likely it is that their relationship will break up, particularly if the woman is already pregnant before she marries or moves in with her partner.

Living together before marriage is not necessarily a good ingredient for a happy marriage, as this just appears to lower the barriers for terminating their marriage. Just as many people who lived together before marriage get divorced as those who did not.

Children affect the happiness of married or co-habiting couples. Both men and women have to work harder at their relationship when they have children, so having a child in the hope of repairing a deteriorating relationship can fail abysmally. Probably the best this strategy can do is to pressurise the partners to stay together for the sake of the child.

A couple's happiness decreases over the first ten years of being together but it increases after their children have left home.

One of the most common problems in relationships is that the husband believes he knows his wife very well (or vice versa) and feels he is in touch with her feelings, when in fact he is not and in a situation such as this a breakdown in communication occurs. If a husband believes he understands his wife, and a wife believes she understands her husband, when in fact they are both wrong, problems are likely to occur. If a man views himself in a favourable light and finds his behaviour satisfactory, it doesn't necessarily follow that his partner will perceive him in the same way. He may take her criticism of him and his behaviour as a fault in her make-up, rather than being able to look objectively at himself.

When one of the partners in a marriage break the rules – either marriage vows or agreed codes of conduct between partners, then the relationship is likely to go into difficulties. This may be the care of children, adultery, financial arrangements or even which one of them washes the car. If one partner trusts the other, as is the basis of most serious relationships, and that trust is broken, the relationship is doomed to failure.

Jim and Kate have been married for 15 years. When they first met neither of them had any educational qualifications. Jim always did basic manual work and Kate, secretarial work for lower management.

During the period of their marriage Kate did part time study and obtained a degree of which she was very proud. Jim felt intensely threatened by the fact that his wife appeared to be "better than him" and started to find it difficult to get erections. Kate's disdain for him then grew, as not only did he fail to give her intelligent conversation but now he was failing her in the marriage bed.

Because she was educated and intelligent, Jim felt there was even more pressure to perform sexually as that was really all he had to offer the marriage, as Kate was in a well-paid graduate job and the knock on effects of his anxiety escalated into almost complete impotence.

To compound this, Jim then started a relationship with a woman who lacked Kate's intelligence and education, and guilt became an added factor to the existing anxiety he was feeling, so his sex life with Kate was completely non-existent, with Jim making no attempts at having a sexual relationship with his wife.

Kate takes the initiative to find a solution to this problem by suggesting they sleep in the same bed but deliberately abstain from sexual intercourse allowing themselves talking and touching in bed which then removes the pressure. Kate is unaware of Jim's involvement with someone else, but the problem becomes resolved as their emotional feelings for each other override the intellectual conflicts, their sex life resumes and Jim ends his relationship with the other woman.

Tiredness or boredom with a relationship tends to cause it to peter out, as does personal conflict in the form of arguments. Unresolvable differences of opinion about important issues are particularly destructive.

One in ten men and one in six women commit adultery but women may be more reluctant to admit to this. Women are more likely to detect adultery in their partners than are men.

During periods of marital shift husbands tend to withdraw and clam up and decline to discuss the problem, whilst women tend to persist with trying to find a solution, which causes the hostility and tension to escalate, creating even more serious problems.

One in three marriages ends in divorce. Over half of second marriages end in divorce: it is often the case that in second marriages people are bringing "emotional baggage" from their first relationship into their second, and often there is a deep rooted desire for the second partner to compensate for the failings of the first spouse.

Peter and Sheila were married for 15 years and had three children together. During the period of their marriage Peter was very frivolous with money and not a particularly good father to their children. Eventually they divorce and Robert becomes a stepfather to their children. Sheila has very high standards for how she wants Robert to behave with her children and the things she wants him to do with them. Sheila feels her children have missed out on good fathering and subconsciously believes it is Robert's duty as her new partner to provide them with all the things that Peter failed to do.

Sheila also finds herself checking Robert's bank statements and money in his wallet to see how much he is spending on himself. Robert is aware of this and also resents how he is expected to be "superdad" to children who aren't even his.

To compound the issue Sheila also has a very over-idealized perception of her own father which makes her standards even higher for Robert.

Sexual dissatisfaction is a major source of unhappiness in marriage leading to arguments and extramarital affairs. The frequency of sexual intercourse appears to have little or no relationship to marital satisfaction. It seems that the quality of the sexual interaction is the most important aspect.

Research indicates that a large percentage of people, in fact, nearly a half of people interviewed in a sex poll, claimed that their sex lives were unsatisfactory. It may be that people compare themselves unfavourably to an illusion they hold about others people's sex lives. Possibly TV and film are to blame in that sex can be portrayed as a profoundly orgasmic experience for both people, whereas in real life very many people have problems becoming aroused or reaching a climax.

The feelings that people have for each other do not necessarily predict a good marriage or partnership. Often arguments can cement a marriage or partnership. If these revolve around the distribution of tasks or requests for things to be done for one partner, who will then reciprocate, then the arguments are more a form of negotiation than conflict.

It is very much the case in present times that people choose not to "tie the knot" but prefer to co-habit, but they will still face the same joys and challenges that conventional marriage bring.

Divorce

"Matrimony is a reversed fever; it starts with heat and ends with cold"

German proverb

"Divorcee" is rarely a term that divorced people choose to use to describe themselves. It smacks of failure, although in reality it often describes a person who has had the courage to terminate a failed marriage. A particular problem for the divorcee is that society still tends to be organised in couples and divorced people can either find themselves feeling uncomfortable in social situations, either because they are self-conscious about not being with a partner or because they fall prey to the matchmaking attempts of well-meaning friends.

Marriage breakdown and divorce involves creating a new identity for the newly separated person and their whole pattern of life can change.

During the period of a relationship that has been legally and socially verified through marriage, bonds of attachment, not surprisingly, are built up between partners. People become emotionally attached to each other by virtue of the fact that there is history between them, particularly the joint experience of shared activities and interests, and important occasions such as Christmas and holidays.

Couples with children have even more emotional history between them. If either party looks back at his or her life over the period of the relationship they will find that the memorable events are the shared experiences of family life and these are parts of one's life that cannot be erased. This is particularly the case for people married for a very long while.

Being divorced often causes a sense of failure, even in people who are deemed to be the "innocent" party. Divorcees invariably find that their financial status changes for the worse after divorce. There is also the need to re-identify their social status, as they are now single rather than part of a couple. A divorcee is also likely to go through the selling of the matrimonial home and the purchase of single person's property – another added strain to the stress of terminating a marriage.

Divorcees with children now find themselves having "single-parent" status, which can bring with it a social stigma as well as the adverse effects of having no shared responsibility for the children or conflicts over access. After living as a couple, divorce can bring loneliness and lack of "in house" support in times of physical illness or mental strain.

People with rigid, defensive personalities and people with psychiatric problems are most likely to be divorced. Age, race and religious differences create low marital harmony, as does the presence of children and pre-marital pregnancy.

Men with a high need for orderliness are more often divorced than men who are relaxed and easy going. Men who see themselves as extraverted and invulnerable tend to end up in the divorce courts, as obviously they have little insight into their behaviour.

In the first year of divorce children from broken families are more oppositional and obstructive, more aggressive, lacking in self-control, more easily distractible distracted and demanding than are the children of intact families. These children are believed to suffer from depression and psychological disturbance, such as excessive feelings of their own guilt.

People become attached to the idea of being married. The state of being married carries with it a lot of assumptions. Merely the wearing of a wedding ring shows the outside world that this person is not sexually available and has made a long term commitment to another person who feels the same way about them.

Most married couples share routines in everyday life, however autonomous and independent they are, and the very nature of living under the same roof as another person offers us a more enriched life than if we lived alone. The shared routines of marriage are believed to be the major cementing force in a relationship.

Although the act of getting married is associated with ceremony; a ritual in which sets of guidelines are laid down, society does not provide couples with divorce ceremonies and there are few guidelines laid down about the correct way to divorce which can often be a very messy business.

The road to divorce

It takes between 18 months and 2 years for a marriage to be emotionally dissolved. When a couple divorce it is believed to be a six-episode drama. The *emotional divorce* comes first when the marriage partners uncouple and become either emotionally hostile to, or distant from, each other. The legal aspects of the divorce are then played out in the court system. Where children are involved, the co-parental divorce involves making arrangements for child custody and access. The economic divorce involves settling property and financial issues.

The *community divorce* then ensues, which relates to the social and friendship networks built up over the period of the marriage. Finally the 'psychic' divorce occurs, which means redefining oneself as a single person.

Various stages of dissolving a relationship have been identified. First one party feels dissatisfaction with the relationship and starts to seriously consider the costs of separating. They will evaluate the partner's behaviour and decide whether it is felt that person is pulling their weight in the relationship. They will imagine what it would be like to live with someone else and ponder over whether to say anything about the dissatisfaction or just keep quiet. (This is known as the intra-psychic phase).

If no improvement takes place the dissatisfied party will move on to the dyadic phase of breakdown where they may feel so strongly about their dissatisfaction that they will confront the partner and initiate discussion about the state of the marriage, expressing their feelings and looking for some feedback.

The dyadic stage of a relationship breakdown is probably the most crucial, as in the case of one party being dissatisfied, (usually it is the woman who instigates divorce proceedings for unreasonable behaviour), and the other party being satisfied with the marriage or relationship, (men being found to benefit more from the state of marriage), then there is the opportunity for a reconciliation to be attempted, problems discussed and behaviour altered so that the relationship can continue but on better terms.

If the other party refuses to accept that they are behaving unreasonably or even refuses to discuss the matter at all, then the dissatisfied partner will reach the stage of being resolved to break up the relationship and then the focus of their discussions with their partner will relate to how they will separate and what their respective situations will be after they have separated. This is known as the social phase of relationship breakdown, and they will discuss the state of the relationship with family and friends, focussing on her the partner's shortcomings and deciding which friends they will keep after the break up if some are shared friends.

At this stage they may make a last ditch attempt to save the marriage by suggesting they receive relationship counselling. If this fails, the couple then separates and the process of rebuilding their individual lives gets underway. Usually an intense psychological post-mortem is carried out and a suitable account of what led to the break up is formulated and circulated. This is known as the 'grave-dressing phase'.

Jan and David lived together in a small rented flat four years before they got married and both enjoyed a lot of freedom in the relationship. Jan is interested in the Arts and Politics; David enjoys sport and socialising. After their marriage they bought a house and things continued much the same as before, but before long Jan began to feel that David's commitment to home improvements, joint outings and social occasions with mutual friends was not as she had expected and hoped for and realised that David had failed to mature, expecting within marriage to live the life of a single man.

After the birth of her first child Jan expected more help around the house and with the baby. She also expected some company and conversation in the evenings feeling a need for social contact, finding baby talk with other mothers not enough. David's refusal to acknowledge that he spent too much time on his sporting activities and in the pub was, in Jan's view unreasonable, and a failure on his part to consider her needs.

Many rows ensued where Jan would confront David with his lack of interest in family matters, and the relationship deteriorated even further when Jan realised how much money he was spending on his personal leisure activities, when she was struggling to buy essentials for the house and the baby. Their sex life petered out and became almost non-existent. At this stage Jan started to consider the pros and cons of separating, balancing the social and financial restrictions of being a single parent against the strain of living with a partner towards whom she felt antagonistic towards. Her refusal to meet David's sexual demands created even more tension but she felt unable to make love with a man who offered her so little in the way of personal or emotional commitment.

After serious consideration Jan confronted David with her feelings about her isolation, loneliness and exhaustion at coping unassisted with the demands of a child and said that if matters did not

85

improve she was prepared to divorce him. She asked him for some commitment to improvement.

David was hard- pressed to see why she felt so aggrieved, and reacted by accusing her of being sexually frigid and having overemotional outbursts, insinuating that she was suffering from some type of neurotic disorder rather than a general dissatisfaction with his behaviour.

Jan now felt that David had no commitment to their family unit or their marriage and started to openly vocalise her complaints about him to her family and friends. She made one last last-ditch attempt to get through to David in his way out to a squash match, but he dismissed her criticism as nagging.

Jan then consulted a solicitor and asked David to leave the matrimonial home pending a divorce. David was initially upset and distressed, appearing to have no idea of how Jan felt but complied, complaining to his own family and friends that he has been kicked out for no good reason and that his wife must have another man lined up.

Divorce often occurs after the infidelity of the husband, most divorces being initiated by the wife.

John is a compulsive womaniser. Shortly after his marriage to Angela he embarks on an extramarital affair. Angela feels betrayed and angry and looks to her own shortcomings to explain his behaviour. They become reconciled but soon the pattern of behaviour is reinstated and John is discovered being unfaithful again. Angela constantly looks to herself, criticizing herself in an attempt to explain why John treats her so badly. She feels disappointed and depressed and her confidence has been destroyed.

86

The reality is that John, who is the second child of four, has always perceived that he didn't get enough love and attention from his mother and has spent most of his adult life looking for the unconditional love he feels she failed to give him. There was always competition for her attention and affection by his brothers and sister and she often played one child off against the other in order to control their behaviour. She would emotionally reject John in favour of his brothers and sister when he was misbehaving.

Angela takes this stance with John when she discovers his affairs and reinforces the childhood scenario of emotional rejection for bad behaviour, but this has the effect of exacerbating the problem.

John's problem is deep-rooted in childhood and although therapy may not necessarily cure the problem, it can offer insight into it and so allow him to attempt to control his behaviour.

Angela decides that the state of her marriage is totally the fault of John and instigates divorce proceedings.

Divorce is a big step to take and the consequences can be dire. This is particularly the case where children are involved, as there is often conflict over maintenance payments and access rights. It also happens that couples who were friends of the divorcing pair now regard the newly divorced person as a threat to their own marriage. Loss of friendships and a sense of social isolation results.

Divorced men in particular appear to have a higher risk of road accidents, are more susceptible to illness, are more likely to commit suicide and have a higher risk of being murdered.

There is no doubt, however, that for an unhappy person trapped in a disastrous marriage, divorce is the only solution to their distress.

Chapter 4
OUR SEX LIVES

"What is it men in women do require? The lineaments of gratified desire.
What is it women do in men require. The lineaments of gratified desire."

William Blake 1757-1827 Epigram

Darwin believed that we evolved from a single-sex species and that humans are inevitably "bi-sexual"; in that men have atrophied breasts and women an atrophied penises, (the clitoris), the large lips of the female genitals being smaller replicas of the penis and testicles.

Testosterone is responsible for the sex drive in both sexes. Females have small amounts of testosterone and production of this starts in girls as young as eight years old.

All human beings start life as a female and secretion of testosterone creates the male embryo.

In the case of Androgen Insensitivity Syndrome, the male foetus cannot metabolise testosterone so an abnormal female grows. These "girls" fail to menstruate and need to have testicles removed but can be successfully brought up as girls. It is believed that Joan of Arc had this syndrome.

Hormones are believed to be responsible for behaviour. Women who have excessive levels of testosterone in their bodies from the foetal stage have unusually formed genitalia and grow up behaving like boys. Between the ages of three to eight years, girls with excessive levels of testosterone play with cars and trains and toys usually associated with boys and tend to have great strength.

Influences on sexuality – What Freud said

According to Freudian theory a person's sexuality is formed during childhood when the child passes through a series of psychosexual stages. The first occurs in the first two years of life when the infant is believed to derive a certain degree of erotic pleasure while feeding at the breast. The infant can then become fixated on the breast, either through over-indulgence or deprivation. This can influence that child's later sexuality.

Around the time of pot training at about two years old, pleasure is focused on the anus and bad handling of the child by the parents can create guilt feelings about anal eroticism which can create sadistic tendencies in later life.

At the time of the Oedipus complex age (four years), when a boy fears castration by his father for desiring his mother, psychosexual fear can arise. It is believed that the female genitals remind the adult male of how he subconsciously believes he would look if, indeed, his worst fears had been realised and he had actually been castrated.

Freud believed that after the age of five the child's sexuality remains dormant, being re-directed into affection and general non-sexual activities. Sexuality re-emerges at about the age of twelve, sooner or later depending upon the age of the onset of puberty.

Repressed sexuality produces nervous tension rooted at the time of castration anxiety which originates in early childhood. Firstly the child shows interest in his genitals and the mother threatens castration ("don't touch them or I'll cut them off"). She can often recruit the father in the process. Secondly, the child fears castration as a punishment for desiring his mother.

The job of adolescence is to revisit and rework the Oedipus complex and shake off the emotional and sexual problems of childhood. Degrading women is a male defence against castration anxiety. Fear and hate are defences erected against anxiety and panic.

Powerful sexual conflicts often appear around puberty mainly left over from the Oedipus/Electra complex. Pubescent girls, realising that their mothers still have sex with their fathers, can feel jealous and believe that their fathers prefer their mothers because they have larger breasts. This feeling is reinforced in later years when they perceive their husbands and boyfriends to appear to be obsessed with women with large breasts, thus invoking the reaction 'he loves her more than me because her breasts are larger'.

By the same token the pubescent boy, when he realises that his father still has sex with his mother, can feel the same sense of sexual inadequacy, only this time relating to the size of his penis. This in turn is reinforced by women's sex magazines showing men with large penises.

Pornography – who is repressed?

"Popular" pornography tends to use performers with abnormally large breasts and large penises as though intended as a substitute for viewing parental sexual activity through the eyes of a child. Sublimation of early incestuous desires can take the form of men fantasising about women dressed in nurses uniforms (a symbol of maternal authority) and women fantasising about men in policemen's uniforms (a symbol of paternal authority). This material must surely meet the need for what Freud called "pubescent scopophilia" – the desire to watch the parents copulating. In pre-civilised times watching parental sexual intercourse was probably the way pubescents learned about sexual activity and acted as a catalyst for them to engage in their own sexual activity.

Other types of pornographic films use actors who resemble pubescents themselves, the women often being dressed in girl guides outfits or school uniforms and the general theme of the content emphasises the 'naughtiness' of the sexual activity portrayed.

It could well be stated that pornography is used by the sexually repressed in an attempt to relieve sexual conflicts that have lain dormant since childhood. Puberty is the catalyst that brings them to the fore and this motivates sexual behaviour.

"Girlie" magazines often show the women posing on hands and knees – the 'lordosis' position, a stance used by primates as an invitation to intercourse – the 'come and get me' pose. These pictures may satisfy the conflict between desire for sexual intercourse with an attractive woman, the fear of that desire, and the object of the desire.

Sexuality is in the mind – the most powerful sexual organ and a person's expression of their sexuality is a product of the way they think. The ability for ideas to be sexually arousing is a multi-million pound industry.

D.H. Lawrence described pornography as "an attempt to insult sex" preferring a romantic approach.

"... and the man felt a sense of peace as he entered the woman he desired"

"Coming to the fire, he sat down and turned towards her. He put sprays of fluffy young oak under her breasts and the weight of her breasts held them there. Then among the oak leaves he put a few bluebells. He twisted a spray of bryony around her arm, poised a primrose in her navel and put primroses and forget-me-nots in the hair of her mound of love. There she was, with odd sprays of flowers and leaves on her naked body"
John Thomas and Lady Jane – D.H. Lawrence

This is at one end of the spectrum of sexual literature; the other being the content of very basic material contained in some publications.

Obviously the purpose of pornographic material is to sexually arouse but other effects have been noted. According to research by Iowa State University, men having watched a sexually explicit film displayed heightened aggressive behaviour and this aggression was just as likely to be directed against men as well as women. Also, over 70% of men reported the desire to have sex after having watched erotic material.

People who scored highly on sex guilt were noted by Dr Patricia J Morokoff to be less aroused by watching erotic material.

After looking at "girlie" magazines and films, men tended to rate their female partners as less sexually attractive than they did prior to looking at the pictures.

The mating game

Desmond Morris describes several categories of sexual behaviour displayed by humans.

Pair formation sex assists in the creation of a pair bond, the uniting of male and female. *Procreation sex* is purely for the purpose of reproducing the species. *Pair maintenance* sex is a means whereby a couple reinforce their sexual commitment to each other by making love regularly. *Physiological sex*, which can probably include masturbation, is a mechanism for using sexual activity as a release from tension.

In exploratory sex, sexual partners discover their own and their sexual partners needs, whilst *occupational sex* is an anti-boredom device. *Commercial sex* involves the promise of sexual activity for money – such as stripping, magazines and films and the purchase of sex for money.

Morris described *status sex* which is concerned with dominance. When chimpanzees indulge in sexual activity the female displays her rump to the male and lowers her head, which can be construed both as an invitation to mate and submissiveness. It acts as an indication of her 'subordinate status'.

In the status sex game, Morris theorizes that because gay men are not interested in women they are not impressed by the conquests of their "straight" brothers who often try to impress each other with tales of sexual conquest. To their heterosexual counterparts they cannot be defeated by the usual rules of the game and so they become ridiculed.

The telling of sexual jokes is believed to be a sign of mild sexual insecurity. Morris believes that the essential property of status sex for sexually inferior men is the degradation of women in the form of prostitution, pornography and striptease. The more sexually inferior the male, the more degrading material he will require.

Sexual satisfaction in a relationship is dependent on the quality of the relationship. It is likely to be very difficult to enjoy sex with your partner if you have feelings of hostility.

Freud believed the lower classes to be sexually free and liberated, and the middle classes uptight and repressed about sex. He believed that intelligence sublimates basic instincts such as sex.

Men are believed to feel intense conflict about women's sexuality, and also their own, and learn to dread their feelings. Consequently, strong sexual feelings are associated with the possibility of death – hence the male "post-orgasm" is called "le petit mort" (little death). Men can often seek to repress female sexuality to reduce their own anxieties.

Sexism is often a result of internal conflict. Many men feel that women are lacking in the ability to be logical, intellectual and reasonable and this is likely to be a psychological strategy with their fear of female sexuality.

Cultural Influences

Men in western culture tend to be aroused by large breasts, buttocks and hips – in their fantasies at least – which is likely to be rooted in basic biological programming: The choice of mates having these characteristics by the prehistoric male had good survival value for his genes, ensuring the successful bearing and nourishment of his young. Obviously civilisation has come a long way from viewing women as empty vessels for the male seed and vehicles for the production of the young, but in primitive times survival of the species would have been paramount.

What constitutes attractiveness varies from culture to culture and a Balinese woman compared to a Western woman would look positively boyish with her narrow hips and small high breasts.

Western women report being attracted to lean muscular men with small firm buttocks. Balinese men, compared to western men are positively feminine looking, particularly being almost hairless, their facial hair being so sparse that it can be plucked rather than shaved.

Sexual behaviour has been noticed to differ between different cultures. Margaret Mead studied primitive tribes. In Samoa, New Guinea, the Arapesh tribe are a gentle agricultural society where both sexes are gentle, caring and cherishing. In contrast, in the Mundugumor tribe both sexes are ruthless and aggressive and the men display "ultra macho" behaviour. These men are extremely competitive with, and hostile to, each other, even to the extent of killing their infant sons. Rivalry for the women of the tribe involves a great deal of competition and fighting.

Most men have difficulty in communicating with each other about sex. Much of male sexuality focuses on the purely physical aspects of copulation and very many men are concerned about the shape and size of their penises, their performance and a certain degree of power or control appears to be evident in male sexuality.

Orgasms

Males reach the peak of their sexual performance level in their teens. It is not uncommon for adolescent boys to indulge in mutual masturbation and this does not predict future homosexuality. A study of sexuality carried out by Kinsey some years ago revealed that 37% of men admitted having experienced orgasm through homosexual masturbation as a teenager. The frequency and intensity of the male orgasm starts to drop from around the age of thirty and the ability to achieve multiple ejaculation also reduces. Erections can be maintained for an average of half an hour in the teens but decreases with age. A man of 70 years can only maintain his erection for seven minutes.

Women's sexuality tends to be affected more by environmental influences than men. During a woman's life it is likely that she will find her sexual desires, needs and responses change according to the time of her menstrual cycle, whether she is pregnant or not, the age of her children and the approach of and completion of the menopause. Some 80% of women report no change or an increase in their sexual desire around the time of the menopause. It is often the case that a woman's sexual desire is strongest in her thirties and forties.

The average time for a woman to be aroused from 'cold' is around 40 minutes and she tends to be much more dependent upon all over stroking and kissing than men who tend to focus most of their sexuality on the penis. Clitoral stimulation appears to be an essential part of a woman's orgasm although Freud described this as an "immature orgasm", the vaginal orgasm being the sexual climax of the mature woman. Women with high IQ's tend to fantasise about other men and other sexual activities whilst having sex with their partners.

Research seems to indicate that women enjoy a continually improving and fulfilling response to skilled love making as they get older, usually peaking in their late thirties and forties. This may be the influence of hormones or just the result of learning to get to know and enjoy their bodies, combined with an increased confidence to express their needs and wants to their sexual partners.

The Kinsey report documented that 13% of heterosexual women admitted having reached orgasm through mutual masturbation as teenagers.

Homosexuality

What constitutes "normal" sexuality can differ from one person to another. The law generally states that most things are permissible between consenting adults – a far cry from twenty years ago when heterosexual anal sex and homosexuality was illegal. A further progressive move is the recent precedent which acknowledges rape in marriage.

Homosexuality and lesbianism have been described as a "narcissistic neurosis" in that the object of that desire is the person himself – like Narcissus who fell in love with his own reflection. More liberal thinkers consider homosexuality and lesbianism to be an alternative lifestyle, whereby an individual makes a conscious decision to have a partner of the same sex.

Freud described the formation of homosexuality as stemming from a child's early experience. Crucial to a child's concept of its sense of 'self' is identification with the same sex parent and the child will model themselves on the father or mother, wishing to be like the person they admire.

According to Freud it is believed that gay men have a great subconscious fear of being 'reingulfed' by their mothers during sex and so feel inhibited and cannot give full expression to their sexual desires. Men who are '(s)mothered' are likely to be gay as their experience of 'reingulfment' will be highly developed. This, combined with a strict 'castrating' father, may be the basis for homosexuality: if the mother threatens castration as a punishment for masturbation every time the child reaches for his penis, he will make the subconscious association between castration and women.

Research has shown that male homosexuals tend to have hostile and remote fathers and over protective mothers, which gives some credence to the theory that these men identify with the sex they perceive as having the better qualities.

Psychologists at the University of California have identified certain circuits in the brain which are thought to be responsible for sexual behaviour. These are believed to be formed before birth and influenced by the male hormone testosterone. The theory is that these circuits have a strong biological influence on sexual orientation which may be controlled by heredity. The brains of male homosexuals appear to be different to those of male heterosexuals. An area in the mid-brain (the hypothalamus) has been shown to be smaller in homosexual men than it is in "straight men" and closer in size to a woman's.

The US Cancer Institute claims a possible genetic predisposition to homosexuality. A specific gene for homosexuality has not been discovered but certain DNA markers on the 'X' chromosome of homosexuals are specific to men of their sexual orientation. The implication is, therefore, that the predisposition to male homosexuality may be inherited through the mother. Of 76 homosexual men interviewed, 13.5% of their brothers were also homosexual which is six times higher than would be the case within the general population which is 2%. More gay uncles and cousins were found in the families of the mothers of gay men than on the father's side. The researchers believe that this discovery provides a 95.5% certainty that a gay man's biological makeup predisposes him towards homosexuality.

Male homosexuals often claim that they have always had strongly feminine traits – playing traditionally female games and lacking the desire for rough and tumble activities usually thought to be traditionally male behaviour. Researchers grade sexual orientation into a number of categories ranging from exclusively heterosexual, to exclusively homosexual, but there are very many people who are heterosexual who occasionally find themselves attracted to members of the same sex. Gay men tend to be poor at maths and better at skills generally considered to be feminine.

Studies have shown that most homosexuals desire a steady love relationship and tend to choose these over casual liaisons. They are also looking for affection and companionship.

It is believed that lesbian relationships are more likely to resemble best friendships but with the addition of romantic attraction. Lesbians on the whole are more likely to be in a steady relationship than gay men and are more likely to be sexually exclusive than gay men. Lesbians tend to place greater importance on emotional intimacy and equality in the relationship than gay men. In homosexual relationships the decision making tends to be age related. Most men know they are homosexual by the age of 17.

Homosexuality and heterosexuality both encompass a broad spectrum. There are many men and women, happily married and with reasonable sexual relations with their spouses, who indulge in homosexual and lesbian behaviour when under stress and feeling emotionally weak. Some men and women are exclusively homosexual or heterosexual only finding members of the same sex or opposite sex attractive.

Gender perception and the expression of 'maleness and femaleness' can be a feature of one's culture. In the Tchambi tribe of Papua, New Guinea, the women are dominant and the men are submissive and emotionally dependent. The women hold the economic and social power whilst the men take pleasure in dressing flamboyantly in flying fox skins and arranging their hair in delicate curls. The women court the men when they are dressed this way. Mohave Indian transvestites mimic pregnancy and childbirth.

The Buzz

It is a phenomenon that people who have conducted extra marital affairs report that once they have moved in with new partners and settled down to day to day living, they start a new affair just for the sense of danger and excitement it would bring. It is obvious that the excitement of planning the illicit meetings and the fear of discovery create arousal which stimulates sexuality.

Adrenalin pumping through an individual's body could be understood by the brain to be fear, anxiety, anger or sexual arousal depending on the situation in which the person finds themselves. Interpretation of our bodily states can be dependent on environmental influences. The bodily sensations of fear and anxiety may be construed as sexual arousal in the presence of an attractive companion.

In experimental situations participants have reported strong feelings of sexual attraction to each other in anxiety provoking situations. An example would be a couple meeting on an unstable suspension bridge high above a canyon, and this could account for the excitement and exhilaration people feel when conducting illicit love affairs. It is very likely that if these people were to meet under more conventional circumstances they would cease to be so excited. Meeting in a non-arousing way would lose its appeal.

Sex Problems

The most common type of sexual dysfunction is male impotence, and when physical causes have been eliminated, the source of the problem can often be traced back to highly restrictive families who equate sexuality with immorality. Impotence, therefore, may be caused by social conditioning which associates sexual arousal, sexual activity and sexual enjoyment, with fear, guilt, threat or pain.

Often impotence itself creates sexual trauma, particularly when this has occurred during early attempts at intercourse. This can then be incorporated into a man's mental framework that he is a sexual failure, rather than just the product of nervousness and inexperience. The ability to have a good sexual relationship is then hampered.

Sexual abuse in childhood also can damage a person's ability to have a good a sexual relationship in adulthood and it is estimated that over 50% of women who become prostitutes have been sexually abused during childhood – many having a sense of lack of worth, only being good for 'one thing'.

Sexual anxiety can be created if one partner perceives their partner's sexual responsiveness as a command to perform. The anxious partner then focuses attention on their sexual failure which starts up a vicious circle. Anxiety can create sexual failure and sexual failure can create anxiety.

A couple with sexual difficulties will often seek therapy, and a useful strategy which therapists use is to forbid the couple to engage in intercourse but encourage them to kiss and pet. Once the importance of performing to orgasm is removed then the problem seems to resolve itself.

Vaginismus is a common sexual problem in women, where the walls of the vagina contract when penetration is attempted. This is mainly psychological in origin and clinical Psychologists often treat this condition with relaxation therapy. This phenomenon is often found in women with sexually restricted upbringings, and with a fear of intimacy on many levels.

Vanessa has had a very strict Catholic upbringing and is still very sexually repressed. She is 23 and is still a virgin – her attempts at having sexual intercourse in the past have failed very badly as she suffers from "vaginismus" which means her vagina contracts at the onset of penetration.

She has always had a morbid fear of sex, having had it heavily ingrained in her during her convent school education that sex is associated with guilt. She has a poor relationship with her mother in particular who frowns upon anything of a sexual nature. She feels that her mother is watching over her when she attempts to have any type of sexual relationship with a man.

She has been with Gordon for two years and he has at times been so frustrated at her inability to have successful intercourse that he has on several occasions attempted to force penetration (which makes him feel guilty and remorseful). Vanessa then becomes so distressed that she seeks professional help.

Vanessa's therapist puts her into deep relaxation and obtains penetration of her with a vibrator and over a period of several sessions, the therapist manages to "desensitise" her to objecting to being penetrated.

With time and patience Vanessa and Gordon manage to achieve a satisfactory sex life.

Women who cannot achieve orgasm are generally taught how to relax, explore their own bodies, and then masturbate to orgasm using erotic material or fantasy.

Psychotherapy and counselling have been of use to many women experiencing sex problems.

Psychological stress, whether in the form of personal problems or financial and work related worries, can create a lack of interest in sex or failure to perform. A very common problem with couples is that due to inhibitions, they are unable to communicate to each other their sexual needs or desires.

Sexuality can often become distorted. Fetishists are fixated on their first intense sexual experience which is associated with an inanimate object. Some analysts believe that an infant or child masturbates in the presence of a fetish object, often shoes or rubber wear (a view of the mother's shoe or whilst wearing plastic pants) and develops a sexual bond with an object rather than with a person. The important point about fetishes is that the adult's sexual desire is linked to a non-human object rather than to a human being.

The Rapist

When 'normal' sexuality is transgressed the sexual object becomes changed. The vagina is replaced by the mouth or the anus. According to Desmond Morris, rapists perpetrate total domination and degradation of their victims; the writhing and facial expressions of pain displayed by the victim are similar to those of orgasm. The rapist is believed to lack the ability to create sexual pleasure and so he creates sexual pain. Visual rape occurs when flashers expose themselves – attempting to shock and shame their victims.

The rapist obviously has deep-rooted problems about his sexuality. Being unable to come to terms with media images of 'sexually available' women and the stark reality of sexually unavailable women, he steals what he can't acquire by socially acceptable means. Rape is mainly about power. The rapist is likely to have deep-seated sexual conflicts stemming from the 'anal stage' (2-4 years) possessing strong conflicts about desire and danger. It is likely that he simultaneously desires and fears the victims of his brutality. In all probability the unconscious shame and guilt that accompany his desires, combined with self-loathing, low self-esteem and fear of rejection prohibit him from forming and maintaining normal sexual relations.

According to some theorists, sexual transgression is discovered in every neurotic person. Paranoia is believed to be an attempt to fend off excessively strong homosexual impulses. Obsessional neurosis is often characterised by the pressure of excessively strong sadistic sexual impulses and the symptoms serve as a defence against these wishes.

Neurotic people with a tendency to brood are believed to have a strong desire to look at, touch and explore others' sexual organs. This is often displayed by a fear of touching and obsessional cleanliness.

Perverse sexuality is believed to be nothing more than the magnification of infantile sexuality split up into its separate parts.

Sexuality is a fundamental part of each individual, both human and animal – a straightforward mechanism for reproducing the species.

Distorted sexuality causes child abuse, violent crime and relationship problems.

Western society has created a highly complex and complicated set of attitudes as to what is a basic human need, an expression of warmth and affection and an aid to a stable relationship. The commercial sex industry is one of the most lucrative in the world, and is in the main condemned by feminists who deplore the debased images of women, and call for improved sex education and openness of discussion of the subject in the public domain.

Attitudes to sex have altered dramatically over a period of time, particularly regarding women's needs. Women are much more sexually demanding than they were 50 years ago and this is probably due to the influence of the media, particularly modern women's magazines, which have taken the lead in confirming their readers' attitudes towards expecting a more satisfying sex life with multiple orgasms.

Chapter 5

EVERYDAY LIFE

"Life is a great bundle of little things"
           Oliver Wendell Holmes (1809-1894)
           The Professor at the Breakfast Table

Food and Overeating

Obesity is believed to have a number of causes. The number of fat cells a person has is fixed very early in life. The brain strives to keep fat cells fed. It is difficult to manage this type of obesity as failure to keep these fat cells nourished creates an impression in the internal mechanism that the body is starving.

In adults of normal body weight, persistent overeating can cause the body weight to creep up but this can usually be dealt with effectively by cutting down on the amount of food that is eaten. Obese people tend to respond to the availability of food and it's attractiveness in terms of taste, as opposed to responding to hunger pangs.

Some people find that they turn to food in times of stress as "comfort eating" but if the causes of the stress can be dealt with or the symptoms managed in other ways, this overeating can be satisfactorily cured. Over-fullness is often associated with emotional well-being.

Obese people tend to eat according to meal times rather than when they are hungry; they let the clock on the wall rather than their body clock tell them it is time to eat. Obese people have been noticed to gulp their food rather than eat it slowly. Dieting in the conventional sense of eating a restricted range of low calorie foods seems to fail as 97% of people who lose weight on a calorie controlled diet soon return to their old body weight.

Dieting tends to make people 'food conscious' as being on a diet can create a constant awareness of food and possibly an increased desire for 'forbidden foods'. Excessive dieting can cause physical ailments and it is evident that the body needs a wide range of foods, including fats and carbohydrates to function properly.

Contrary to popular belief, fat people also have a fast metabolic rate and burn off energy more quickly in order to feed a larger body. Thin people tend to be fidgety and jittery and burn off calories in this way.

Although our eating habits are a great determinant of our weight, it has been found that heredity plays an important role. Research at the University of New Orleans has shown that identical twins reared apart had virtually identical weights, although these twins had completely different eating habits. A substance (called melanacortin) found in the brain is believed to prevent obesity and a lack of it has been found in the brains of obese people.

Obviously, there are emotional factors connected with overeating, particularly what are known as "comfort foods". It has been discovered that chocolate contains a substance (called phenyethylalanine) which is a chemical secreted by the brain when we are in love.

Eating has psychological benefits – the enjoyment of a piece of chocolate, a good meal and a glass of wine etc, can produce an immense sense of well being. If someone is overweight then probably the best course of action is for them to eat normally but reduce the size of their meals, taking care to eat when they are hungry rather than by the clock and to eat more slowly. A method that has been used to control food intake is for a person to eat what they like, but it must not overlap the inner rim of the plate.

Whether or not someone is perceived as obese depends mainly on fashion and culture. In some societies plumpness is considered extremely sexy and Rubens spent a great deal of time painting women, who, by modern standards, are fat.

Preoccupation with body size and weight can create a vicious circle and can lead to problems such as bulimia nervosa, the conflict between the desire for food and the simultaneous rejection of it – the bingeing and dieting syndrome. In this disorder there may be a certain amount of psychopathology in that food could be linked to love. The bulimic may well be caught in a conflict between their desire for food, with its associations of comfort, nourishment and survival, and their rejection of these things in their quest for autonomy.

A person suffering from an eating disorder will need clinical therapy and this may focus on the bulimic's intense personal conflicts.

Smoking

Smoking has been linked to lung cancer and other serious illnesses. Research has indicated that in pairs of identical twins where one smokes and the other does not, both are equally likely to die from lung cancer. The Japanese smoke almost twice as many cigarettes per person than the British, but the Japanese lung cancer rate is only one fifth of the British lung cancer rate.

Mark Twain claimed he never smoked more than one cigar at a time, never smoked when asleep and said giving up smoking was the easiest thing he ever did, he had done it thousands of times.

It could be argued that there are different types of smoker who display a need for a cigarette in different situations and circumstances.

The stimulation smoker is more likely to light a cigarette when doing a difficult job, finding it helps to keep them alert and improves their concentration. The 'indulgence smoker', smokes when comfortable and relaxed and likes to sit back and enjoy a cigarette, particularly after meals.

Social smokers smoke in social situations, they offer and accept cigarettes and feel confident and sophisticated when smoking with others.

The 'sensory smoker' enjoys having a cigarette in their mouth, likes the feel of it and enjoys lighting it up. They enjoy watching the smoke as it is blown out.

The addicted smoker deems it unbearable to have run out of cigarettes, feels a gnawing hunger to smoke if too long between cigarettes and doesn't know what to do with their hands without a cigarette.

The "automatic smoker" also smokes without being aware of it, and can often have more than one cigarette burning at a time.

Smoking can also said to be a type of "comfort blanket" for the "oral" personality type, who is fixated on their mouth in times of stress; the cigarette being a type of adult dummy.

There is no doubt that smoking is harmful to the health and is the cause of cancer and many respiratory and cardiovascular problems. The cost of cigarettes is also prohibitive.

Loneliness

In a large sample of people studied, 26% reported feeling lonely in the few weeks leading up to their being interviewed. Intense loneliness is something that is experienced by most people at some time or other.

There are different types of loneliness:

Trait loneliness is a stable and persistent pattern and this is usually created by the people themselves. They will claim to feel lonely in any situation however friendly and welcoming the people.

State loneliness is a temporary feeling resulting from a specific situation such as separation or a move to a new environment.

The crucial feature of loneliness is the difference between what we are doing and what we expect to be doing. We can feel lonely in a crowd, yet be perfectly happy alone with our own company.

Truly lonely people generally have a sense of being helpless and feelings of panic. They are also bored and restless and have low self-worth. Chronically lonely men tend to act in an aggressive and hostile way towards other people. They tend to treat their female partners badly, being very punishing towards them, and many violent men, particularly rapists, have very strong traits of loneliness and social isolation.

Teenagers, particularly, feel lonely at weekends because this is a time during which they expect to have more social contact. In fact, for most people loneliness is perceived more in the context of what they would like to be doing as opposed to what they are actually doing. Obviously being alone at Christmas and New Year

111

would create more intense feelings of loneliness; than would being alone on a weekday afternoon.

Lonely people tend to be self-absorbed, negativistic and ineffective in their interactions with strangers. These people often attempt to offset their feelings of loneliness with "busy-busy" activities or by taking vigorous exercise. Also "retail therapy" (spending large amounts of money on oneself) is believed to be a strategy to offset loneliness.

Shy people tend to be lonely and programmes have been set up to improve the social skills and self-perceptions of people with feelings of extreme loneliness. These focus on improving self-esteem and communication patterns to encourage better social interactions.

Lonely people tend to avoid eye contact and are reluctant to reveal intimate details of their personal lives. Contact with women by both sexes tends to reduce feelings of loneliness.

All of us will feel lonely at some time in our lives but this is something which usually passes. Intense and persistent loneliness can have very serious consequences and the risk of suicide cannot be ruled out.

Prejudice

A stereotype, where we make sweeping generalisations about people based on one small piece of information, can best be described as a widespread, oversimplified package of beliefs. Prejudices are strong feelings about negative stereotypes.

A prejudiced person will have a small amount of information about someone, say the colour of his skin, and will have a negative concept of them. They will also behave towards this person in an objectionable way. Prejudiced people score highly on fascist scales and this is usually reflected in their political views.

Studies of prejudice and anti-Semitism in America have produced a profile of an individual likely to have prejudiced and anti-Semitic attitudes. This person is known as the *Authoritarian personality*. Typically, the Authoritarian personality denies any conflict between their parents, thinks their parents are perfect and have a favourable impression of themselves. The Authoritarian personality tends towards racist and fascist viewpoints, often making statements such as "homosexuals are no better than criminals and should be severely punished" and "all blacks should be repatriated". They also believe ideas such as "it is human nature to be warlike" and "people can be divided into two distinct groups – the weak and the strong". The main characteristic of the Authoritarian personality is prejudice, an extreme attitude that is resistant to change, and which appears to meet a deep rooted psychological need.

The prejudiced person is generally emotionally insecure with an inferiority complex and sees the object of their prejudice as a scapegoat on whom they can project the repressed anger and hostility contained within them and which usually stems from their childhood. Because of their strict upbringing they were unable to express negative emotions as a child for fear of punishment.

A person's attitudes are a facet of their personality. Narrow-minded people have been observed to have "low cognitive complexity" (a stereotyped package of beliefs) and are likely to be prejudiced. Being closed-minded and dogmatic reduces an individual's ability to form new belief systems.

Prejudiced people displaying fascist type attitudes usually have very little knowledge and understanding about the people against whom they are prejudiced. The prejudiced person is closed-minded. The prejudiced Authoritarian personality dislikes ambivalences, preferring to see things in black and white – something is either one thing or another and these people are unable to see both sides of an argument. They tend to project their own personal repressed anger onto minority groups and their accusations against these people could be described as purely an extension of their own unfavourable traits.

There appears to be a phenomenon which, under competitive or threatening conditions – such as in times of economic recession and high unemployment, people tend to oversimplify their views about others and look for a group identity as a defence against perceived threats to their well-being and status. In times of economic crisis there appears to be a rise in rightwing thinking with neo-fascism emerging to take advantage of many people's fears. There appears to be a tendency to see black people and other ethnic minorities (known as "out groups") as scapegoats on which to focus blame for lack of work, poor housing and inadequate health care. Well-off Asian and Jewish business people are usually the first to be targeted in an economic recession rather than the prejudiced person looking for personal, social or political solutions to his plight.

Aggression & Violence

A centre exists within the brain which is believed to be responsible for creating aggressive urges (the amygdala). Work done with animals has shown that disorders of this part of the brain can affect levels of aggression. Very limited research has been carried out on humans, but there is no conclusive evidence to support this idea.

Another theory of what causes aggression relates to chromosomes. It has for some time been believed for some that it is the Y chromosome which makes men more aggressive than women, and some years ago it was noted that very many violent prisoners displayed the 'XYY syndrome', in that they had an extra male chromosome.

A lot of research into aggression has focussed on environmental influences, particularly those of TV and film in influencing, promoting or legitimising violent and aggressive behaviour.

A Psychologist called Bandura did some important research into the effects of children witnessing screen violence. He made two short films, featuring an inflatable life life-sized doll, which were shown to four-year-olds. One group of the four year olds was shown a film of other children being pleasant to the doll, playing with it and talking to it. The other group of four-year-olds was shown a film where the doll was physically abused by children. The children tended, when presented with this life-sized doll, to re-enact the same behaviour they had seen on the film; particularly, the children who watched the violent film were witnessed being violent to the doll.

Delinquent boys in particular showed increased aggression after seeing violent films, claiming they gave them "a buzz".

Nathan Martinez aged 17, from Salt Lake City, murdered his step-mother and half sister in October 1994 after seeing the film *"Natural Born Killers"* 10 times, and there was speculation that his behaviour had been influenced by this film.

Research was carried out on a sample of two hundred children, half of whom watched violent films and the other half who had seen non-violent films. The children imitated the violence they had witnessed.

A Forensic Psychiatrist stated that violent patients of hers claimed they had been motivated to commit acts of brutality after watching violent and pornographic films.

Other research has shown that gratuitous violence on screen, particularly where the victim appears to suffer few injuries from an assault, has the effect of desensitising the viewer to the effects of violence.

It is generally believed by Psychologists that television and film violence has a detrimental effect on the viewer, particularly when the victim is dehumanised. This is particularly the case relating to people in concentration camps with their heads shaven. Where the results of the injury are not obvious to the viewer, then they will not internalise the effects on the victim.

Konrad Lorenz, who mainly worked with animals, but also projected his theories onto humans, claimed that human beings are by nature highly aggressive and that their natural condition is that of the warrior. He believed that aggressiveness is important in competing for limited resources. Violence is often spontaneous and could be precipitated by hunger, sexuality and self-preservation and that instinctive aggressive energy builds up and demands discharge.

Freud stated that the impulse to destroy ourselves is so strong, we must destroy some other person ("The Death Wish"). Conflict with the Life Instinct results in aggression being displaced on to others, but aggression can also be 'sublimated' into sport and adventurous activities.

It is also believed that people who are "over-controlled" repress their anger and the pressure of this builds up. This can give support to the idea that violent criminals should be given physical activities whilst in prison and young offenders offered the opportunity to engage in adventurous activities.

Morality

There are three types of morality that govern people's behaviour according to the level of their personal development. This is usually formulated during childhood.

Pre-moral reasoning is characterised by a primary concern with satisfying that person's own needs and self-interest and these people will seek self-gratification at all costs, their only constraints being the fear of punishment.

Conventional reasoning includes concern for others and an almost unquestioning acceptance of established authority.

Principled reasoning takes into account the welfare of others and reflects self-chosen laws based on ethical principles.

People at this level respect the law but see it as a human invention, in that it is there to be broken, if necessary, to fit in with higher moral values. These values are acquired in later childhood and adolescence and require intelligence and maturity.

The "morality reasoning" test applied to decide on the level of conscience was devised by American Psychologist, Lawrence Kohlberg, and requires a decision on the following story.

A sick woman is dying of cancer and only a certain drug can save her. The chemist is selling the drug for 10 times what it costs him,

117

and the woman's husband has only half the asking price. He tells the chemist that his wife is dying but the price is not lowered. The desperate husband breaks in and steals the drug.

The question asked is should he have done so and why?

A person's answer to this question is deemed to indicate their level of moral functioning.

Morality is believed to be learned in childhood, based on parental authority and child rearing methods. Eli Sagan, an American Psychologist, claims that behaviour similar to premoral reasoning (avoiding punishment) is formed as a result of paternal authority but the real conscience is formed by good maternal nurturing.

He also believes that behaviour similar to pre-moral reasoning is formed as a result of paternal authority, whilst the true conscience is formed by good maternal nurturing.

Unemployment

The reactions to unemployment are similar to those of bereavement. The first response may be shock, disbelief and numbness. The more a person has enjoyed their job and the more friendly and sociable the working environment, the more intense will be the reaction to its loss. For many people, apart from the sense of purpose and financial reward, the work-place can offer opportunities for friendship. This is known as a "closed field", whereby it is difficult not to interact with people at work and social contact is virtually guaranteed. An unemployed person then suddenly finds themselves cut off from an instant source of social interaction and then has to rely upon an "open field" for daily social contact. The "open field" relates to the people one comes into contact with on a daily basis and is more distant and transitory than that of the closed field. Opportunities to form friendships with the postman, shop workers and other trades people are fairly remote and these interactions are normally restricted to small talk.

Although unemployment is often the result of redundancy, bankruptcy of companies or economic recessions, the suddenly unemployed person tries to make sense of what has happened and is often self-analytical and critical, attempting to gain mastery over the situation to prevent it happening again.

The unemployed tend to have higher rates of mental ill health; they are prone to feelings of helplessness, often blaming themselves for their own job loss, particularly in companies that trim their work forces. Unemployed people are more likely to commit suicide or to become alcoholics. Unemployment often brings poverty and it is difficult to be involved in social gatherings when money, even for basics, is in short supply.

For people who were previously in high status jobs and earning high salaries, their self-concept may well have revolved around work, status and social competitiveness. Being unemployed and living on state benefit can be devastating.

The initial reaction after the loss of a job can be that people feel elated. They can develop a sense of having a well deserved holiday, particularly if they have received a good pay-off and feel optimistic that another job is just around the corner. As job seekers continually meet dead ends and the rejection letters start to arrive frequently in the post, the sense of optimism is replaced by pessimism, particularly if debts are starting to build up. As the length of the unemployment increases so a sense of fatalism, hopelessness and apathy can set in and the job seeker can sink into a state of depression.

Marital and family relationships very often suffer. There is evidence to show that children are dealt with more harshly, sexual relations diminish and marital harmony is affected during the period of unemployment.

Generally, unemployment causes loss of social contact, disrupted family routines, poor psychological health, as well as obvious financial hardship.

Success

A person's ability to achieve their goals depends on the general view they have of their chances of succeeding. People with a weak fear of failure tend to set themselves realistic targets which they are capable of achieving. People who have a strong fear of failure set themselves goals so low that they couldn't possibly fail, or so high that they could not be expected to reach that level of success.

The way we manage people

In the workplace management plays an important role, and a crucial factor in group atmosphere lies in leadership style.

Researchers have identified three different types of leadership style.

"Laissez- faire" leaders basically just let things go along without intervention and give no advice or direction to the people of whom they are in charge. The people under their jurisdiction are neither productive nor satisfied and tend not to work well.

At the other extreme are the *autocratic* leaders, who exercise rigid control over people under their jurisdiction, not allowing any dissent and expecting their workers to abide by the rules to the letter. People led by autocratic leaders tend only to pay lip service to rules and regulations and tend to break them at the first opportunity.

People who use *democratic* styles of leadership are believed to be more intelligent than autocratic leaders. Democratic leadership has been found to be the most successful way of managing people and this involves getting a group to discuss what needs to be done and deciding how to achieve the objectives with guidance from the leader.

Individuals compare themselves with others in order to establish or validate their behaviour, or attitudes, particularly where objective criteria are lacking. A similar phenomenon occurs in group settings and every group needs to maintain a positive social identity relating to other social groups and this is likely to be the case in work place settings. Groups provide their members with identification of themselves.

Niccollo Machiavelli stated that the best way to handle people is to tell them what they want to hear and that anyone who completely trusts anyone else is asking for trouble.

People can be divided into Machiavellians and non-Machiavellians, relating to their ability to manipulate others. Research has shown that intelligent people who use Machiavellian techniques are very successful in business, although if these techniques are used in their personal lives they could have disastrous effects: low I.Q. Machiavellians tend not to be taken seriously.

In 1990 John Mayer and Peter Salovey in Universities in America defined an ability felt to be particularly valuable in the business world called "Emotional Intelligence".

They believe that to be emotionally intelligent it is necessary for people to be in touch with their own and other people's feelings. Emotionally intelligent people are adaptable, co-operative and have good self-control. A positive attitude towards life and the ability to cope with stress are also essential.

In the book *"The Millionaire Mind"*, Thomas Stanley reported on the findings of a survey taken of 733 multi-millionaires throughout the United States. They described five main factors they believed were most responsible for their success:

- *Being honest with people,*

- *Being well disciplined,*

- *Getting along with people,*

- *Having a supportive spouse,*

- *Working harder than most people.*

In sports psychology the technique of mental rehearsal of the game is often used and the players are asked to imagine overcoming the types of problems that usually arise in sports matches. The traditional psyching up of players before an important match is believed to be detrimental to their chances of winning. Prior to a big game players are likely to be anxious and over-aroused. A pre-match pep talk will just increase anxiety levels and produce a poor performance.

Chapter 6
OUR LIFE STAGES

"Even such is Time, that takes in trust,
Our youth our joys our all we have.......
When we have wandered all our ways
Shuts up the story of our days."
                                    Sir Walter Raleigh 1552-1618

Erik Erikson was a Danish Psychoanalyst who developed a theory of human growth and development. Erikson originally studied under Freud but rejected Freud's emphasis on the biological and sexual aspects of human development, believing instead that personal development is a life long process and is governed as much by a person's social environment as it is by biological drives. He claimed that humans pass through critical stages of ego development during their lives.

Becoming a well-adjusted person

At birth and during infancy a small baby is totally dependent upon the parents for satisfaction of its needs and its ego. Development can take the course of two directions, depending on how the parents satisfy the child's needs at this stage. If the child overcomes its insecurities and trusts the parents to satisfy its needs the child will develop the "ego quality" of *hope* and its experience of adults in its environment will be positive and beneficial, shaping the way the child sees the world.

During early childhood good parenting will allow the child to shrug off any sense of shame and self-doubt they may have, so that they may become confident about their abilities, be autonomous and independent and develop the "ego quality" of "*will*" which permits them to channel their skills and abilities effectively.

The play age between three and five years also combines the biological drives children feel towards the opposite sex parent (Oedipus/Electra complex) with social circumstances such as pre-school experience and mixing with other children. Competent parental handling during this time will diminish negative emotions, such as the guilt children often feel for their sensual feelings. The qualities of initiative, being able to plan to get what they need and want in an acceptable way, will then produce the "ego quality" of "*purpose*".

The school years are characterised by the conflicting feelings and experience of being as good as one's schoolmates or being inferior. If the child is encouraged and given confidence, any sense of inferiority is overcome and the "ego quality" of "*competence*" is produced.

At adolescence, which Erikson regards as the crisis stage, the development of an independent personal identity occurs. Creating this sense of self often entails rebelling against the parents. If the adolescents can overcome their "role confusion" this will establish a personal identity and the "ego quality" of "*fidelity*" is produced. The young person can then be true and faithful to friends and ideas based on a mature set of values. This is crucial to establishing the mature adult personality.

Often this fails to happen as the '*identity crisis*' during adolescence has not been resolved. It appears that many people spend their lives in perpetual adolescence, pleasure seeking, yet isolated, and never achieve the depth of personality required for satisfactory personal and sexual relationships. Adolescents desperate to achieve autonomy and independence from over restrictive parents may turn to drink, drugs and promiscuity which can set the tone for their adult life.

The Capacity for Intimacy

The early twenties bring the need to form intimate relationships in emerging adulthood. This is a time when young adults tend to commit themselves to partnerships even though they may call for significant sacrifices and compromises. The intimacy which is required for a committed relationship is very largely dependent on the satisfactory establishment of an identity during the adolescent phase. While sexual relations may be involved, Erikson thought that the key issue in establishing the intimacy of young adulthood is the mutual search for shared identity, which is finding oneself by losing oneself in another.

True sexuality requires psychological intimacy with a loved one. This, combined with physical intimacy, produces a different and more mature sexuality than casual encounters. It is the grounding for a stable and mature adulthood where the ability to love another person and to enjoy being needed, is a desirable quality.

Many individuals may remain immature throughout adulthood, unable to face up to life's responsibilities and duties. This can take the form of unwittingly reacting against marriage partners in the same way that an adolescent would react against parental values, and destroying their chances of personal happiness with a life partner.

The failure to establish this sense of intimacy in adulthood is a growing sense of isolation and self-absorption.

Young adulthood is the first of three broad phases into which Erikson separates adult life and the successful triumph of intimacy over isolation results in the capacity to love.

Five crucial stages in the development of adult maturity and the capacity to achieve good and lasting adult relationships have been identified.

Firstly, *good basic nurturing* is essential to human development. Secondly, *identification* with a parent should take place. This is part of finding out who you are and what your values are by wanting to be like the person you love, admire and respect. This usually happens with the same sex parent, but starts in infancy with the bond between mother and child. *"Defensive identification"* is hoping to gain the power and the status of a person, defending yourself against your own lack of power and status.

Thirdly, *generalisation* occurs. The initial identification takes place within the family but then new role models can be sought outside the family, possibly teachers, or other relatives.

'Abstractions' arise next and these are usually in adolescence when the young person becomes interested or involved in political and social institutions and starts to take a philosophical stance on life. A further phenomenon of adolescence is the fifth stage of development into adult maturity and that is the questioning of parental authority.

When these abstractions have been successfully resolved in a positive way, then the young person can move on to become an independent mature adult, with good personal relationships.

The individual then starts to function in the outside world, encountering all the pleasures and challenges that adult life can bring, and the effects they will have on that person.

Middle Age

The middle years of adulthood, the 40's to the 60's, are characterised by Erik Erikson as the conflicting qualities of Generativity vs. Stagnation. The essence of Generativity is the concern in establishing and guiding the next generation. Adults can pass on their skills and knowledge and what is important is the sense of giving oneself without expectation of return. Becoming a parent doesn't necessarily guarantee the quality of generativity developing. An adult who doesn't develop generativity retreats instead into a boring preoccupation with themselves and becomes their own infant and pet.

At this time married couples often regress into an obsessive need for intimacy with each other as if they were each other's children. The ability to avoid stagnation and cultivate generativity, (that is concern for one's children, grandchildren and the young, in general), produces the ego quality of care.

For most people the mid-life stage involves an assessment of our lives so far. Have they been happy, successful and productive? Can we learn from previous mistakes so that the future can be better? Middle-age is often the turning point for many of us to look closely at our jobs, careers, education, financial status and marriages. These influence important decisions about what the second phase of our lives should bring.

The Menopause

The menopause is a significant milestone in a woman's life. She has now reached the end of her ability to conceive and bear children. Whether she has children or is childless, the completion of the menopause biologically removes from her any chance or control she has over fertility. The menopause brings with it hormonal changes but many women "sail" through the menopause with very few symptoms and welcome the freedom from the risk of unwanted pregnancy and the expense and inconvenience of sanitary protection.

However, 40% of women suffer from depression; 30% from sweating; 25% from insomnia; 20% from fatigue; 15% from skin changes; 10% from headaches, and these symptoms may persist for up to one year. Anxiety and hot flushes are also experienced by very many women, but less than a quarter of women experiencing symptoms feel they are severe enough to warrant seeking medical help.

The menopause may well have a more social than physiological significance. Freedom from the risk of unwanted pregnancy may cause many women to become more relaxed about embarking on extramarital affairs. Often the menopause coincides with the children leaving home and so can increase a woman's sense of independence and freedom - 80% of women report that sexual responsiveness is either unchanged or increased.

Apart from physical health problems, which can affect some women at this time, such as brittle bones (or osteoporosis), society's perception of post-menopausal women can well have the more profound influence. A post-menopausal woman returning to work may well expect to be employed in a senior and well paid position, which she feels is in keeping with her experience and maturity, but she may lack the necessary skills after spending so much time at home. The menopause often comes at a stage in a woman's life when she may be assessing her satisfaction with her life so far. Her relationship with her husband may have changed; she may feel that she has matured and he has not – that she has outgrown him and her previous reasons for continuing the marriage, often being financial support for her children, are now gone as they have grown up and now lead independent lives.

At the time of the menopause women often feel psychologically young but experience a conflict between this and looking their age. Female clothing is often construed as a demonstration of sexual availability and a 50 year old woman may be giving off the wrong signals if she dresses in clothes intended for a younger woman. Many menopausal women become competitive with their adult daughters possibly feeling threatened by their youth and beauty.

Often the emotions a menopausal woman experience are similar to that of a young girl emerging into womanhood and perhaps could be described as puberty with wrinkles!

The Mid-Life Crisis

The mid-life crisis is well documented, and men, as well as women, suffer symptoms such as insomnia, depression and weight gain. Men often notice that their body hair increases and their voice deepens, rather like at puberty, and often mood swings are evident. The male menopause has been well documented and it has been the subject of much debate as to whether it is a biologically or socially constructed phenomenon.

The Swiss Psychologist, Carl Jung, who specialised in the treatment of middle-aged patients, said that culture was the goal of the second half of life and that schools for 40 year olds were needed. Many men around the age of 45 regress into adolescence, start to dress in teenage style clothes and adopt teenage habits. This is associated with decreasing testosterone levels, which affect behaviour.

Peter has been married for 30 years and has a comfortable home, a pleasant wife and two grown up sons in professional jobs. Suddenly, out of the blue, he announces to his wife that he is leaving her for another woman, packs his cases and leaves, despite the fact that they have been living harmoniously for very many years. He sets up home with Patricia, and they begin a very active social life of parties, holidays, meals out and visits to the theatre. He changes his style of dress from dull and conventional to the latest fashion and believes he feels like a new man, young, alive and enjoying himself.

Soon the novelty wears off as neither of his sons will speak to him and the divorce costs him dear. He realises that he runs a very poor second to Patricia's job, her own children, her hobbies and extended family life and now realizes realises that all he has had is a fling. He is disillusioned and would dearly like to return to his old life, but doesn't want to lose face.

Research has shown that many people experience a psychological shift in their forties. Men appear to develop a more feminine side, becoming more nurturing and intimate, whilst women develop a more masculine side becoming more assertive and ambitious. With marriage partners this can lead to either disharmony or very productive living, depending on the degree to which the partners experience this shift. It may be that by the time a man reaches 45 he has reached the peak of his work achievement, going as far as he is likely to go. He may accept this and be content to jog along from day to day at work in a comfortable routine without the pressure of going for promotion, salary rises and the need to prove himself.

His wife, most likely having brought up a family and possibly having developed new skills and educational qualifications, may see her new role in the outside world, feeling entitled to have a slice of the cake her husband has been eating from for so long and takes on a responsible well-paid job. In this situation both parties can benefit from the shifted role experiences. The woman will feel satisfied with her new status in the world and her husband can realise the feminine side of his nature by becoming more involved in the domestic area. They can also both benefit from the increased wealth and the opportunities it affords.

Problems may arise if the male ego is insufficiently well developed for him to accept this shift. If he has a dogmatic view of a man's role as breadwinner and stereotyped attitudes about male/female roles, then conflict is bound to arise.

People who have experienced financial problems, unemployment and problems within the family often face a crisis at this time, particularly if they feel things will be no better in the future.

Retirement

Six phases in the process of retirement have been described.

In the *pre-retirement* phase the older worker is aware of friends and colleagues retiring and his or her thoughts may turn to their own potential retirement and what this changed lifestyle will offer. Immediately after retirement, the honeymoon phase occurs where the newly retired worker enjoys the new found freedom – both from having to get up at a set time and from the demands and obligations of being an employee.

Once the novelty of being retired has worn off then disenchantment can set in and the retired person can start to feel let down and depressed. For most men work has been the focal point of their lives since leaving school and even during periods of unemployment the concept of paid employment will have dominated their mental life. It can be that a man finds his presence at home during the day interferes with his wife's routine, if his wife has not been in paid employment for many years and has established a life for herself at home. Many women complain that their newly retired husbands "get under their feet" and may also experience demands to drop their daytime activities and reorganise their lives around their husbands.

The *stability* phase of retirement is when the retired person has reorganised for themselves a new lifestyle and is comfortably settled into it. Retired people now know what each day will bring, what is expected of them and what their strengths and weaknesses are.

The *terminated* phase occurs when a retired person starts to suffer illness associated with old age and is unable to pursue their previous lifestyle due to ill health.

Successful handling of the retirement process involves moving into the re-orientation phase and exploring ways of using up one's time productively. At this time a combination of voluntary work and development of hobbies can offer the retired person a new perspective and meaning to life.

Old Age

Old age is the final stage of adult development described by Erik Erikson as a positive state. In old age there needs to be the quality of ego integrity, which is the quiet certainty of who one is, accepting the nature and inevitability of one's own life and not looking desperately for last minute restorations. The elderly person who has developed this quality of ego integrity avoids a sense of despair in their later years by appreciating the richness of the many ways that life can be lived.

Lack of ego integrity is often marked by despair – by an agonised concern about the shadow of impending death. Unrealised goals and unfulfilled potentials can be expressed as disgust with life and other people. Only integrity can balance the despair of a knowledge that a limited life is coming to an end and relieve the sense of despair of facing a period of relative helplessness, which marks the end as it marked the beginning.

Bereavement

When we suffer bereavement there can be a severe shock at the sudden loss of a friend or loved one, particularly if the death is the result of an accident or is premature. There is often a sense of disbelief that this person is no longer with us, combined with a refusal to accept the fact that death is final and the dead person is gone forever. Once the death has been accepted, intense grief usually follows and can be accompanied by anger or guilt. A sense of depression often follows bereavement and the bereaved person needs time to rebuild a life that excludes the deceased. Physical illness can often be a side effect of losing a loved one.

Robert Burton, in his *"Anatomy of Melancholy"*, referred to the experience of bereavement as a "fierce or violent sorrow". The melancholia of a real depressive illness differs substantially from those feelings experienced by someone who has been bereaved. People who have suffered loss through death often feel self-reproach and this is a major cause of depressive illness.

133

After the death of a loved one there is a need to give vent to the feelings of sadness, anger and guilt which have been repressed. If this doesn't happen the grief can then become distorted or delayed. One of the therapies used is "flooding", in which bereaved people are pressed to recall the sight, smell, sounds and feelings associated with the dead person. Counselling in the early days of the loss of the loved one is useful to prevent further problems later on.

Bereavement causes similar problems to those of divorce with the widowed person having to assess themselves as a single person, often after many decades of marriage. Some people report an illusory sense of the continuing presence of the dead person that may be retained for many years.

The loss of a parent through death often sees the re-emergence of sibling rivalries which existed during childhood, whereby the younger child resents taking second place to the first born.

Rose was widowed after 57 years of marriage and Sally, her middle child of three daughters, decides to take care and control of her mother, particularly in view of the fact that Rose has inherited a large sum of money from her deceased husband.

Sally effectively poisons her mother's mind against her other two daughters and the eldest daughter in particular, as she feels her older sister has seniority in the family hierarchy. Mary, the eldest daughter, is cut out and overruled from any decision that Sally makes for her mother. Sally also sets out to divide and rule by trying to cultivate good relationships with her eldest sister's husband and children whilst simultaneously turning her mother against her other daughters with lies and deceit.

134

Rose is in a dilemma, in as much as she loves her three daughters equally but because Sally lives locally to her, feels she must give her loyalty to her as she is dependent on her at the expense of the rest of her blood relatives. This creates just as much emotional distress as the original bereavement did.

Nine components of grief have been identified:

- *Shock*: in the form of numbness;

- *Disorganisation*: an inability to function;

- *Denial*: acting as though the deceased was still alive;

- *Depression*: desolate pining and despair;

- *Guilt*: the person may think they neglected the deceased when they were still alive;

- *Anxiety*: apprehension about the future; fear of losing control of one's feelings;

- *Aggression*: irritability and outbursts of anger at people in the family or even towards the person who has died;

- *Resolution*: life must go on;

- *Reintegration*: a new life built.

Many widows report symptoms of fatigue, insomnia, loss of appetite, weight loss, headaches, breathlessness, palpitations, blurred vision and exhaustion.

Widows who failed to give vent to their feelings of distress during the first weeks of bereavement were significantly more distressed three months later.

The more unsatisfactory the relationship with the deceased when they were alive, the more disturbed will be the grieving process. A Psychologist called Krupp said "if we can learn to live with the living, then we can learn to live with the dead".

The death of a loved one in men often creates the same health problems as they do for divorced men, and it is not uncommon for widowers to die within a short time of their wives.

Apart from the life stages described by Erikson, there may be certain other crisis stages that affect adults at the time of transition into adulthood.

During puberty and adolescence there are profound hormonal changes; the starting of the new school, sexual awareness, homosexual crushes, more self reliance, peer group pressure, concern with activities and fashion and work for exams. The emerging awareness of the opposite sex as potential sexual partners and the girlfriend/boyfriend stage, stage tends to coincide with preparation for examinations that will affect the young person's future.

Pregnancy and childbirth can present women not only with profound hormonal changes but changes in personal relationships, finance and lifestyle. A woman's relationship with her husband may change after the birth of their child. Decreased sexual activity due to the demands of an infant can put a tremendous strain on a marriage, particularly if a new father was previously used to having his sexual needs accommodated. A new mother may lose interest in sex, being preoccupied with caring for her infant, and perhaps fearing the risk of a new pregnancy so soon after giving birth. If she was previously a woman who enjoyed sexual activity with a skilled and caring partner, her reduced sexual desire may cause her distress. The birth of a first child can create a tremendous fear of the unknown: the responsibility for a new life may weigh heavily on a woman who has had no experience of children and little in the way of positive support. A couple's financial status changes after the birth of children: even if the mother returns to work fairly quickly, a large proportion of their earnings are likely to be taken up with child care fees and providing clothes, food, toys, etc, for their child.

New parents often find that their social network changes after the birth of children and there is a certain amount of loss of personal freedom as the baby's needs tend to take precedence when arranging social gatherings. A new mother particularly finds that she loses her independence: personally, socially and financially.

A new mother may also perceive herself as the object of surveillance. Friends, relatives and health visitors will be judgemental about her child rearing methods, passing comment and offering advice about the way she deals with her baby.

The crucial point about personal growth and development is that as people travel through life they leave another piece of childhood behind. They will meet each new problem and challenge with adult mastery, constantly taking stock of their situation and finding mature ways of reaching solutions to their problems.

The late teens and early twenties are characterised by an internal assumption that we are still our parents' property and psychological independence from them can carry penalties. Up until the early twenties (twenty-three being the age at which adolescence is believed to end) most behaviour is carried out as a means of gaining parental approval, or a reaction against parental authority even if these people are in permanent relationships or even parents themselves.

During the rest of their twenties people mature and become more aware of their own abilities and potentials, although parental values will still prevail to some extent in that person's life decisions.

The late twenties and thirties are characterised by simplicity and lack of complications in a person's internal make-up. They have a fair idea of who they are and what they want and tend to feel fairly safe and secure in the world.

The period between thirty-five and fifty is a time when we need to face up to the reality of the world and realise that we can be vulnerable, therefore taking the necessary precautions.

People tend to progress through the life stages automatically but the amount of personal growth they sustain must necessarily depend upon their own personal experience. People who have lived in the same area and worked in the same job for most of their lives may sustain very little personal growth, whilst someone who has had more varied life experiences is likely to be a different person in her fifties than she was in her twenties. They are likely to have developed a deeper understanding of life than other people and have richer and more varied aspects to their personality than people who have had a narrow and limited existence.

Chapter 7
SLEEPING AND THE DREAMS WE HAVE

Sleeping

"…….sleep is that golden chain that ties health and our bodies together"
Thomas Decker (1570-1641) The Culls Hornbook

A third of our lives are spent in sleep. Studies of sleep have been made. At rest with the eyes closed the brain produces *"alpha waves"* and this is known as the hypnogogic state, the state the brain is put in when someone is hypnotised, meditates or does yoga. "Brain waves" were discovered by Richard Caton in 1875 and are measured by an electro-encephalogram.

Five stages of sleep have been identified. *Stage 1* is a light sleep, where the heart rate is slowed, the muscles relaxed and the sleeper easily woken. The *alpha* waves from the previous hypnogogic state are replaced by low-voltage, mixed frequency waves. The sleeper's muscles are relaxed and he is unaware of external stimuli. *Stage 2* sleep lasts for about half the night and the brain's "sleep spindles" are short fast bursts. During *Stage 3* sleep, the heart rate, blood pressure and body temperature drop and the brain produces longer slower waves. *"Delta sleep"* – the stage of deepest sleep, the *fourth stage* of sleep, is often referred to as "healing sleep". The brain produces very slow, delta rhythm waves, and the sleeper has difficulty in waking. This fourth stage of sleep is thought to aid healing and the repair of body tissues.

Sleep is triggered by changes in the brain stem. When this is excited the brain is alert, when it is depressed sleep occurs. The nerve pathways from the sense organs are directly connected to this area of the brain and are directly affected by noise and light, so a sleeper awakens when a loud noise is heard or a bright light is shone. The sleep mechanism is affected by changes in the body's chemical or hormonal levels which fluctuate rhythmically in a 24-hour cycle.

Rapid eye movements

Dreaming occurs in cycles throughout all stages of sleep, although dreams are more easily recalled from the final stages of sleep. Dream sleep has been connected to rapid eye movements which have been observed under the closed eyelids of sleepers who are dreaming. The brain activity during this REM or dream sleep is high and focussed on the cortex of the brain. REM sleep is essential for good mental health. Men commonly have erections during this type of sleep.

Of people woken during REM sleep, 83% reported having been dreaming. Dreams also occur at the onset of sleep and these are known as hypnogogic reveries.

The production of growth hormone begins to rise shortly after the onset of sleep as well as the secretion of the male hormone testosterone. The hormone which is responsible for the release of the female ovum (luiten) and the hormone which is responsible for the production of breast milk (prolactin) are also secreted during sleep.

At the base of the brain (the pons) there is primary control over REM sleep. When this part of the brain is destroyed in cats they begin to act out their dreams.

Episodes of dreaming occur every 90 minutes throughout the night. People deprived of dream sleep make it up later, so there appears to be an innate need for dream sleep.

Dreams can often remove stimuli which disturb sleep by means of hallucinatory satisfaction. For example, if we fall asleep with the electric blanket on we are likely to feel hot and sweaty and dream of being in the jungle or sauna.

There are recorded cases of people requiring such small amounts of sleep that they appear to require virtually no sleep at all, although they still manage to lead busy active lives, without any side effects. One case such as this relates to a retired nurse who claimed to have slept only one hour a night: a claim that was verified under laboratory conditions. Margaret Thatcher, who was Prime Minister for 11 years, apparently ran the United Kingdom on only three to four hours sleep a night. However it is obvious that sleep plays an important role in our physical and mental well being. When we are feeling unwell, through illness or overwork, the body demands sleep and often we have no option but to crawl into bed.

Juveniles and teenagers appear to need more sleep than adults and there is evidence that growth hormone is secreted during sleep. Sleep is important for the relief of psychological stress and for people living intellectually demanding lives. Often these people seek temporary help in the form of hypnosis, meditation or sleeping tablets so that they may shut off for a few hours.

The effects of sleep deprivation are mainly psychological causing stress, debility and irritability, and lost sleep is soon made up. The main physical effects of sleep deprivation are mechanical skills that require accuracy and dexterity.

Sleep profiles change with age. Newborn infants sleep for a significant proportion of each 24 hours, but the elderly need very little sleep at all, particularly elderly men. Stage 4, very deep sleep decreases from the late 30's onwards, leading to a complete absence in old age.

Sleepwalking is believed to be hereditary. It occurs early in the night during orthodox sleep, not during rapid eye movement sleep, so it does not appear to be a product of dreaming.

Lady Macbeth sleepwalked and acted out irrational dream experiences and this is believed to be a manifestation of the "twilight state" which occurs in some forms of mental illness.

Many people report having discovered the solutions to their problems during sleep: hence the advice to "sleep on it" when somebody has a difficult decision to make. The solution to the dilemma probably comes from the subconscious and is likely to be blocked out by the conscious/logical thought processes which prevail during the waking hours. This would indicate that during sleep the brain's function is different to that during waking hours, as borne out by changes in brainwaves detected by electro-encephalograms.

The Dreams We Have

"A dream which is not interpreted is like a letter which is not read"

The Talmud

The philosopher, K.A. Scherner, first described dream symbolism in 1861 when Sigmund Freud was just five years old. He described the human body as being represented by a whole house. *Houses with smooth walls are women and houses with balconies and other protrusions are men. Parents are represented by royalty; brothers and sisters by small vermin. Dreaming of*

weapons, tools and materials, Scherner believed, represented masculinity and femininity respectively.
Various other interpretations of dreams have been made.

Artemidorus (AD138-180) a Greek philosopher stated that to dream of a weasel means that you have a wicked wife, fond of strong drink.

Nostradamus (b.1503) believed that "to dream a cold hand is put to you in bed, and your next news a relation will be dead".

Old Moore's Almanac claims that to dream of grapes means that your husband will be a great singer.

The Modern Dream Book published in 1920 claims that to dream of drinking beer means you will lose a large sum of money, so avoid horseracing.

Dreams in Ancient Greece were regarded as prophetic and this idea is contained in the poems of Homer. It was believed that they may contain prophecy or binding instructions because they "come from Zeus" but they were also felt to have been sent to deceive. It was believed that there is a difference between "significant" and "non-significant" dreams.

"Non-significant" dreams just reflect the anxiety and desires felt by the dreamer during the previous day. "Significant" dreams describe events which could possibly happen to the dreamer. Sophocles described the frequency of men dreaming of sleeping with their mothers and Plato described them as wish-fulfilment. Aristotle felt that the soul exercised special clairvoyant powers which were divine in nature.

What Freud thought dreams mean

In 1900 Freud wrote in one of his most influential works, *"The Interpretation of Dreams"*, that at the bottom of every dream is an attempt at wish fulfilment. Wishes that cannot be expressed directly are censored. Often we dream of people talking in mumbles, or the dream is so jumbled that it appears incoherent; this is a result of the mind's defence mechanisms doing its work. *"Condensation"* of a dream results in it being remembered as a dream which lacks continuity, in the same way as a heavily censored film loses its meaning after scenes from it have been cut.

Freud believed that while the events of the day crop up in the context of dreams, their real significance is that they provide a vehicle for the disguised representations of conflicts and desires rooted in childhood experience. He claimed that dreams have two types of content: the *"manifest* content", which is what the dreamer is aware of having dreamt and which can be highly symbolised; and the *"latent* content" of the dream, which is the true meaning under the censorship.

Someone who dreams of climbing the stairs and entering a room (the manifest content) is, according to Freudian theory, actually dreaming of sexual intercourse (latent content). The manifest content of any dream is deemed to be meaningful.

In 1897 Freud's father died, and he explored the emotions it aroused, working principally with his dreams, seeking out the unconscious processes that formed them. He remembered the sexual feelings he had towards his mother and jealous rivalries with his siblings. He felt that dreams are often symbolic of impulses which are unacceptable at a conscious level and their function is to relieve tension. He believed that dreaming can release the incestuous nature of the libido. Dreams, he believed, have their meaning in the disturbing wishes of the adult dreamer.

According to Freudian theory a dream element is a substitute for the unconscious element which is resisted and this takes the form of symbols. *Loved ones can be symbolised by jewels and treasure. Sexual enjoyment can be translated into a dream of eating sweets.*

The basis of Freudian theory is that human behaviour is instigated by the unconscious mind, the larger part of mental processes being unconscious and which is comprised of desires and wishes which can be of a sexual nature or a destructive nature and which are unknown to the person. The mind uses various ways of preventing those unconscious wishes and desires reaching consciousness. Repression prevents us from being conscious of unacceptable impulses and this is known as a defence mechanism. Defence mechanisms can cause us to sublimate (redirect) our sexual energies into a non-sexual form, e.g. academic work, sport, etc. Denial is a refusal by the conscious mind to acknowledge things which that are true. Access to the unconscious mind, according to Freud, is only possible through hypnosis and the analysis of dreams, when the conscious mind, presumably, is sufficiently inactive to allow repressed wishes and desires to express themselves.

In dreams the interplay between the *Id* (I want) and the *Superego* (You must not) is more than likely taking place on a nightly basis and is free to function without the distraction of constant environmental interference.

Freud noticed that his audiences were amazed by the fact that what instigates dreams are actually evil and extravagant sexual wishes. Anxiety dreams are often the undisguised fulfilment of wishes not acceptable wishes, but repressed ones.

To dream of dancing, riding, climbing or of violent experiences is a distortion of the desire for sexual experience. Sexual intercourse is symbolised by dreaming of ladders, steps and staircases with increasing excitement and breathlessness the higher one climbs. Dreaming of being pursued by wild animals or being chased or threatened in many ways represents an excited sensual state.

Sexual penetration is represented by knives and diving. The vagina is symbolised by pits, cavities, hollows, chests, pockets, cupboards and stores. The vulva is symbolised by snails and mussels; breasts by apples, peaches and fruit in general; pubic hair by woods, forests and bushes. The penis is symbolised by snakes, tall buildings, aeroplanes, rockets and anything that defies the force of gravity.

To dream of playing the piano, of gliding and sliding is the wish fulfilment of masturbation. To dream of having a tooth pulled is a representation of castration. In some tribal societies boys are circumcised at puberty, but in other tribes the circumcision ceremony has been replaced by having a tooth pulled. Birth is symbolised by water and death by departure, e.g. a train journey. To dream of falling often relates to grief or loss. You are letting go but the sensation is distressing, displacing fears that a parent or loved one will leave you.

The real dream of a 15-year-old boy

"I am at the top of a skyscraper with my younger sister and some friends. Also with us is a child called Little Richard who is very small, smaller than the rest of us and whom I don't know. At the top of this skyscraper there is a fairground ride which goes out over the edges of the building. I am on this ride at the top of the building when the carriage comes loose and I jump off it while it is still going. I jump on a ski slope and slide down into a forest.

146

Next I find myself running through alleyways and past warehouses and nurses in white coats. I notice a large limousine driving past and the passenger inside is an attractive female television presenter who used to present children's programmes but who now presents adult programmes. I find a small piece of plastic and call up to the other children that they must jump from the fair ride as it is unsafe and that I will catch them on my piece of plastic. My sister and the other children jump and are caught by the fire brigade but Little Richard jumps down and dies".

The Freudian Interpretation

This 15 year old boy is now physically mature and is at the age where many boys start looking for heterosexual relationships. The skyscraper represents an erect penis (a phallic symbol). The fairground ride symbolises sexual excitement. The jumping onto and sliding down the ski slope is a representation of sexual intercourse and the forest symbolises female pubic hair. The alleyways are vaginas and the warehouses are female bodies – these probably represent the awareness of the amount of girls available to him as potential mates and the fact that they are less glamorous than his ideal. The nurses are symbols of maternal authority, which is the main obstacle for the adolescent male in establishing independence as a sexually active adult.

The celebrity in the limousine is an attractive TV presenter who has probably been a desired woman to the boy when he was a child. She has class, style and status as an "object of desire" and real life has reinforced for him his transition into adulthood by the fact that she now presents adult TV programmes as opposed to children's television. His object of desire now has the possibility of being accessible to him.

The boy's need to rescue the other children from the funfair ride at the top of the skyscraper. There is a combination of fear and excitement associated with this experience which can arouse sexual feelings.

Little Richard, the very small child in the dream, most likely represents the loss of the boy's childhood – he now does not recognise himself as a child. When the other children jump into the arms of the firemen (male authority figures) the small child dies.

What Carl Jung thought dreams mean

Carl Jung believed that dreaming functioned to balance the conflicting needs of the persona (the acceptable projection of ourselves to other people) against the shadow (the darker side of human nature) without outside distraction. Through relating their dreams, the patient furnishes themselves with the most important means of gaining access to the unconscious and disturbing complexes connected with their symptoms.

Jung described the unconscious forces that drive human nature. The personal unconscious is based on an individual's unique experience in the world. The racial unconscious holds the memories and experience of the race or ethnic group to which an individual belongs. The collective unconscious is the sum total of the memories and experiences of the human race as a whole. *"Archetypes"*, which are often found in myths and fairytales, are patterns of instinctual behaviour contained within the collective unconscious.

Jung believed that symbols used by dreamers, for example, dreaming of a Queen (the symbol for the mother) or a King (the symbol for the father), would be common for all human beings of whatever race, creed or colour, originating from the collective unconscious. The mythology of different countries and the various religions of the world would all then tend to have a common theme.

A Jungian dream interpretation takes a more spiritual and mystical approach than a Freudian interpretation, which tends towards a biological/sexual viewpoint. However Jung did describe the *sexual symbolism of dreaming of bulls, donkeys and dancing.* Jung's emphasis was on symbols used by the dreamer to find his or her self, such as dreaming of Christ or the Buddha.

Although he was originally a disciple of Freud's, Jung rejected concepts such as guns representing penises and tunnels representing vaginas and questioned the idea of sexual desire being the be all and end all of dreaming. He claimed that other, non-sexual emotions such as ambition, fear and hate are just as important.

Jung wrote the book *"Memories, Dreams and Reflections"* in which he described dream symbolism.

Dreams of monsters, vampires, dark caverns or being beneath the sea, Jung claimed, relate to our primeval existence which is stored in the collective unconscious – the cumulative experience of all humankind.

Jung believed that *"dreams are able to enlighten people about their inner life and reveal to them the aspects of their personality which in everyday life appear as neurotic symptoms"*.

According to Jungian theory a man repressing his *anima*, (the female side of his personality), is likely to dream of a "succumbus" represented by the traditional "femme fatale", sex symbols, mermaids and nymphs. A man projects the feminine side of his nature on to a metaphorical hook to create a picture of his own perceived femininity. Jung uses the term "anima" instead of the soul.

The animus, (the male side of personality), tends to be represented by a group of men, often depicted in the mind as an assembly of dignitaries or judges, men with power who lay down judgements and opinions. The force of the animus can create an over-active conscience and feelings of inferiority.

He believed that dreams are the force of nature, and that they correspond to people already known, characters in mythology, poetry, books and plays. He believed that "if we meditate on a dream sufficiently long and thoroughly, if we carry it around with us and turn it over, something almost always comes of it". A series of dreams is a better basis for interpretation than a single dream.

Dreams often bring hidden conflicts to light by showing an unknown side of the character. Jung also felt that dreams could have a prophetic nature. People often dream of actual situations which have been concealed from them, the intuitive side of their nature revealing information to them in their dreams

Jung related the dream of a sick 17 year old girl who dreamt she came home and saw her mother swinging from a chandelier. There was an icy cold wind blowing in the room. He believed "mother" to be an "archetype" and referred to the place of origin, to nature, to that which passively creates. It also means the unconscious or natural instinctive life, the psychological realm of the body in which we dwell or are contained. The 'mother' is also the matrix, the hollow form, the vessel that carries and nourishes and it thus stands psychologically for the foundations of consciousness.

The real dream of a 42 year old woman

"I dreamed the Queen came into my local pub and got a job as a barmaid. I was very distressed at this and kept asking her to leave. I didn't feel that pulling pints was appropriate behaviour for royalty".

The Jungian Interpretation

This is a classic Jungian dream in that because of the intense emotions felt about close family members and our relationships with them it is often necessary to dream in symbols. In this case the dreamer has for a long time been concerned about her mother's drinking and also the bad behaviour associated with it.

These concerns then express themselves in the symbolism of the Queen, (the dreamer's mother), and her alcohol related behaviour. In this case, the anxieties are sanitized by the dreamer's mother just being a barmaid, but the dreamer still feels very upset about this being inappropriate behaviour.

Jung also believed dreams to have a prophetic nature. A patient of his described his dream. He was climbing a high mountain and becoming more elated the higher he climbed. He commented on the steep, snow covered slopes and said he felt as though he could climb right up into space. He described the feeling of climbing on empty air and being ecstatic at this experience.

The climber who described this dream was three months later observed to literally step out into the air whilst descending a rock face.

151

Jung believed that dreams could not be dismissed as insignificant episodes.

"Personal dreams" are from the dreamer's personal unconsciousness. The dreamer dreams of real events and situations where known people and places are dreamt of. "Collective dreams", which contain a lot of archetypes the "weird and wonderful" dreams, relate to humanity in general and the experience of being a human being. The understanding of one's dreams can pave the way to self-knowledge. Personal dreams relate to the dreamer's own life whilst collective dreams relate to the society and culture in which the dreamer lives. (In primitive societies these are known as "little dreams" and "big dreams" respectively).

Jung was greatly influenced in his thinking by Eastern mysticism and believed the "Mandala", (a type of magic circle found in eastern religions), occurs in dreams and is associated with strong feelings of peace and harmony, the significance being the ability to find "God" inside ourselves.

Most Psychologists believe that dreaming is necessary for mental well-being and a well-balanced personality.

According to Freud, a nightmare is a dream that has been unsuccessful. In the case of a nightmare, the content is so very threatening that the usual unconscious mechanisms for protecting the ego fail to function and the conscious mind is needed to keep the material under control so the dreamer wakes up.

Plato stated *"good people dream of doing bad things, bad people do them"*.

Chapter 8
PROBLEMS WITH OUR MENTAL HEALTH
& THERAPIES WHICH MAY HELP

"Everything we think of as great has come to us from neurotics. It is they who found religions and create great works of art. The world will never realise how much it owes to them and what they have suffered to bestow their gifts on it".
Marcel Proust (1871-1922) "Remembrance of Things Past"

Up until the 18th century mental hospital were pseudo prisons and performed the function of containing the inmates, rather than offering them any type of treatment or therapy. They were a place of containment for "criminals, idlers, old people, epileptics, incurables of all sorts and the mentally disturbed". "Madwomen seized by fits of violence are chained like dogs at their cell doors and separated by an iron grille. Through this grille is passed their food and the straw on which they sleep and by means of rakes part of the filth that surrounds them is cleared out".

In the latter half of the 18th century Phillip Pinel instigated reforms to mental institutions where inmates were shackled and chained. This is a far cry from the host of therapies and techniques available today.

Psychological disorders affect a great proportion of the population and it is necessary to make the distinction between a 'first stage nervous disorder', such as anxiety, and a serious mental illness which involves an imbalance in the chemistry of the brain and generally prevents that person living a normal life. A person with a mental illness will be treated by a Psychiatrist, who is likely to use drug treatment, possibly in conjunction with other therapies. People with nervous disorders usually manage to lead a normal

153

life, finding various coping strategies and perhaps being prescribed mild medication.

The important difference between a mental illness and a psychological disorder is that the mentally ill person is detached from reality. The neurotic agrees that his fears and anxieties are mainly unfounded and that the problem lies within him, whilst the psychotic truly believes the frightening and hostile world he perceives is real and threatens him personally.

Stress

Worrying is generally considered to be bad for us and is generally believed to be a negative thing. We are biologically programmed to achieve as much pleasure and as little pain as we can. When unpleasant things happen, the centres of the brain which trigger the experience of pain are activated and the experience and emotions associated with unpleasant stimuli are registered in the mind.

There is healthy worrying and compulsive worrying. A person who is concerned that he may have inherited heart disease from his father will have regular health checks. A person who fears unemployment during an economic recession will familiarise himself with the benefit system. A mother who fears for her child's health during a whooping cough epidemic will have the child vaccinated. These are all examples of healthy worrying which produces positive action. Worrying can act as a psychological insurance policy and is more successful than the "it can't happen to me" attitude.

It is an ability to learn by our mistakes which prevents us from making wrong decisions in the future. The purpose of worrying is to prevent bad experiences repeating themselves or to prevent unpleasant situations occurring in the first place by having the ability to anticipate problems and to think out a solution to them before they happen. Generalized worrying creates a state of mild anxiety which can be deemed preferable to having major disasters in one's life.

People who worry for no apparent reason can be described as neurotic. A person who worries about unemployment when jobs are plentiful; someone who worries about having a heart attack when there is no family history of heart disease and they appear fit and well, are examples of obsessional worrying. This can be regarded as neurotic. Someone who worries that Martians will kidnap them, or that their mind is being controlled by outside forces is psychotic.

Profound psychological stress can cause mental breakdown and physical illness, although what constitutes stress can be difficult to define. What one person takes easily in their stride, another person may not be able to cope with. Another phenomenon is called "stress high" where a person does not realise they are in a stressed state, perhaps through having a demanding but enjoyable job. They may enjoy the feeling of the adrenalin pumping through their system, without realising the effect this is having on their health. "Stress high" is often found in people who enjoy energetic sports and become addicted to it. The highly stressed person has such large amounts of adrenalin running through their body that they take it as a signal to be more and more active. What can then happen is that this person, who gets a buzz out of being stressed, will then suffer damage to their immune system or they will suffer a mental breakdown.

The signs of suffering from stress are:

- Feeling guilty when relaxing and not on the go;

- Sleeping problems;

- Muscular tension, causing headaches a stiff neck or a backache;

- Impatience or irritability;

- Difficulty concentrating;

- Eating, drinking or smoking to excess;

- Skin problems;

- Mood changes;

- Having rows;

- Difficulty with decisions;

- Excessive frustration when things go wrong.

- Frequent feelings of panic: i.e. butterflies in the stomach, sweaty palms, dry mouth and thumping heart.

Stressful life events have been given a rating scale. The death of a spouse, divorce, death of a close family member and personal illness and injury have the highest ratings respectively. Children leaving home, being pregnant, having a large mortgage and trouble with the in-laws have a moderate stress rating. Christmas has been given a comparatively low rating.

Experiencing several moderately stressful life events simultaneously can still have the same effect on our physical and mental heath as one very highly rated experience.

People suffering from the symptoms of stress need to attempt to identify the causes and decide which pressures take priority and which ones can be safely ignored. They need to be more assertive and learn to say 'no' to others making demands upon them.

Stress triggers unplanned change. People suffering from a stress-induced illness can have their condition exacerbated by the added pressure that this change in their lives causes. An executive who needs to take time off from work for an ulcer caused by a demanding job can find their recovery impaired by worrying about their work building up while they are away. They will be concerned about the possibility of losing their job, with all of the financial consequences, if they are away sick for too long.

There are links between stress and heart attacks, high blood pressure, asthma, migraine and gastrointestinal disorders.

The physical reactions to stress which have been observed are:

- Alarm reaction – the defensive forces are put on red alert.

- Resistance (sustained) – the body goes into emergency reaction prepared to deal with the danger.

- Exhaustion – the defences are depleted through being stretched for so long.

Humans are biologically programmed to deal with a perceived threat by pumping adrenalin around the body which increases heart rate and breathing providing more blood for the muscles of the arms and legs. The bowels and bladder empty in preparation for dealing with the source of threat.

These patterns are dangerous over a prolonged period and can create health problems.

A person's personality type can affect their health and the health of other people. There is a type A personality who is achievement striving, hostile, competitive and aggressive. This personality type is associated with having coronary heart disease. These people are hasty, impatient, hyper-alert, very tense and intense and can turn a relaxing social occasion into a high pressure, competitive situation.

Conflicts occur when people experience two or more contradictory goals. This can be the choice of two equally attractive alternatives, two equally unattractive alternatives, or the choice between an attractive (but impractical) alternative and an unattractive (but sensible) alternative.

Shift work causes stress by disrupting the body's normal "clock". Shift workers often report experiencing insomnia, digestive problems, irritability, fatigue and sometimes depression.

Energy is increased and heightened emotional arousal creates temporary anaesthesia. People under stress are often impervious to pain. This affects people most severely when they are in a position of helplessness - when they can neither flee nor fight. Reactions to stress also depend on that person's self-esteem and their ability to cope with problems.

The emphasis on reducing stress is on complete physical and mental relaxation. Useful therapies include hypnotherapy. Many hypnotherapists are lay people and practice privately, although some NHS Clinical Psychologists may provide hypnotherapy to their clients. Many hypnotherapists are trained in analysis, which involves psychoanalysis under hypnosis and is used for rooting out the cause of debilitating nervous disorders. They will also practice "suggestion therapy" where the client who suffers from stressful environmental influences is helped into a state of deep physical and mental relaxation. Positive suggestions are then made for their continued relaxation and well-being. Suggestions may also be made for the sufferer to take more control over his or her own life, to be more assertive and to visualise competent handling of stressful situations.

Stress is one of the major symptoms of modern living and often it is impossible to avoid life's problems. Cultivating an appropriate attitude to stressful situations, which one is powerless to change, can be useful in stress management. Becoming agitated in a traffic jam serves no useful purpose, nor does impatience in a shopping queue.

Generally a change of mental attitude towards the problems life can bring is the most useful strategy in limiting the amount of physical and psychological damage sustained.

General Neurosis

General neurosis is an exaggeration of a normal person's personality. The most common cause of psychological disturbance is the "first stage" nervous disorder. A neurosis can cause a usually shy and introverted person to become withdrawn and depressed. This is an extension of their normal personality and they will always be aware of their condition. The neurotic person is in contact with reality and realises he or she has a problem (often the result of environmental stress exhausting the nervous system) and only one part of the personality is affected. The sufferer may be much more irritable or bad-tempered than usual;

an emotional person may cry more. Neurosis, a psychological disorder, is very different to a psychosis, a psychiatric disorder. Psychotics are prone to delusions, usually of grandeur. These people often claim to be important characters from history, such as Napoleon or to have established empires in large countries. Neuroses are generally treated with counselling, psychotherapy and mild tranquillizers/anti-depressants. Psychotics are very often hospitalised and treated with strong drugs.

From the ages of 6 to 8 the majority of experiences and mental impulses of the first years of life are subject to repression and thus "forgotten". In families with high levels of conflict and serious problems, children under the age of 8 years tend to blame themselves for problems within the family.

A human being's first choice of love object is primarily incestuous but these urges are usually diminished around the age of seven years. Puberty rites in primitive tribes are intended to release boys from incestuous relationships with their mothers and reconcile them with their fathers. In the case of neurotic men, the son is bound all his life to his father's authority and is unable to transfer his feelings to people outside the family; this is also true for women unable to free themselves from their mother's psychological control.

Unsuccessful resolution of the Oedipus and Electra complex is one of the most common sources of guilt by which neurotics are tormented.

Phobias

Some theorists believe that phobias are learnt during childhood by the child witnessing a parent reacting with fear to a certain object or situation.

Other Psychologists believe that phobias are a left over from the early stages of human history when people who quickly learned to fear heights, strangers and separation, which in primitive times were dangerous situations, were more likely to survive. This idea seems to be supported by the fact that there is little evidence of people being phobic about modern inventions. (The area of the brain which creates phobias is different to the part which produces genuine and realistic fear).

There is a very extensive range of phobias:

- *Xenophobia* is a fear of foreigners;

- *Arachnophobia* is a fear of spiders;

- *Belonophobia* is a fear of sharp objects;

- *Scopophobia* is a fear of being stared at;

- *Spheksophobia* is a fear of wasps;

- *Acrophobia* is a fear of heights;

- *Algophobia* is a fear of pain;

- *Astraphobia* is a fear of thunder and lightning;

- *Phobophobia* is a fear of fear;

- *Hodophobia* is a fear of travel, a phobia that Sigmund Freud experienced.

The most common phobia is *agoraphobia* which is responsible for 60% of all phobic disorders. It is predominantly a female complaint and is considered to be a fear of being alone, anywhere, which is possibly a form of separation anxiety stemming from childhood. The agoraphobic is afraid that something will happen to them and there will be no-one there to help.

Agoraphobia is a condition where the sufferer fears being away from home, being in crowds, being confined, going shopping and travelling on public transport. In these situations the agoraphobic experiences a state of panic which can often feel like a heart attack, or the sufferer may feel that they will pass out or die. This condition is more common in women between the ages of 18 and 35.

Mary has a morbid fear of supermarkets. As soon as she goes into a supermarket she becomes overwhelmed by fear. Her legs start to tremble, her heart pounds, the palms of her hands sweat and she feels on the verge of collapse. She feels the need to escape this environment as a sense of profound urgency. The intense feelings of panic she feels convince her that she is having a near death experience.

People who suffer from agoraphobia tend to come from families with a history of instability and where at one extreme they may have been extremely overprotected or at the other extreme, neglected as children. These people have a generally anxious temperament which is aggravated by stress in the environment.

One of the treatments for phobias is something called systematic desensitisation, which was developed by Joseph Wolpe in the 1950's. The patient is required to practice deep muscle relaxation, (which is incompatible with a state of anxiety), and then gradually to imagine herself themselves up a ladder of anxiety, visualising situations, starting with the mildest anxiety provoking situation, and ending up with the most threatening, so that a strong association between deep physical relaxation and highly threatening psychological stimulation can be created.

Another method of desensitisation requires the sufferer to be gradually exposed to the object of the phobia. People with a fear of spiders would start by being shown a picture of a spider and then would be progressively exposed to the real thing, first in a glass container, systematically coming into closer contact with the spider until it can be touched without too much anxiety.

It is also believed that a phobia is just a generalised anxiety, which an intelligent person attempts to identify by associating it with an object or situation, which they can then avoid.

Another way of treating phobias is "flooding", whereby the sufferer is subjected to facing his or her fear straight on and experiencing, under controlled conditions, the feelings of overwhelming anxiety that this produces.

It is likely that we are biologically programmed to be "emotionally vigilant", as the person who leads their life in a totally relaxed and fearless state is also being reckless with their safety. Some degree of anxiety for one's own well-being causes us to make the right decisions and to take care of ourselves.

In many cases a phobia may be a displacement of a real feeling; the phobic may be reversing their emotional reaction to a situation or object. A fear of knives or sharp objects may be a repressed desire to stab somebody. A fear of heights may be a repressed desire to jump off a cliff or tall building from a great height and a fear of leaving home may be a repressed desire to run away and not come back; but which the sufferer will constantly reject because of the consequences.

In contrast to systematic desensitisation to reduce anxiety levels a method called "flooding" may be used. The patient is told to lose themselves in an imaginary anxiety-provoking situation and allow themselves to become overwhelmed with panic. A claustrophobic will be told to imagine they are locked in a confined space and to fully experience the emotion associated with it. The intention is for the sufferer to get in touch with the irrationality of their phobia. Another therapy, cognitive therapy, attempts to persuade the sufferer to make a conscious rejection of false belief.

Eating Disorders

Eating disorders were first observed in the late 19th century by William Gull who described anorexia nervosa in 1876. Bulimia nervosa was identified much later in 1920's. Eating disorders affect between 1 and 2 people in 10,000 so are not common, but should be taken very seriously. Some of the explanations given for eating disorders include the symbolic avoidance of pregnancy, a desire to revert back to a childlike body, (particularly as the periods stop and the breasts shrink when the body is starved of food). This illness could also be construed as being a power mechanism, where the only control an anorexic or bulimic has over their life is their intake of nourishment.

Anorexics tend to overestimate their body size. Young women appear to make up the majority of sufferers of eating disorders, although it is now being seen among men. Being the daughter of an overweight and dieting mother has been observed to be associated with incidences of anorexia and is more prevalent in women involved in businesses where thinness is an integral part of one's job such as fashion modelling and some areas of athletics and dancing. In 80% of cases, anorexic patients are hospitalised and sometimes drug therapy can be used.

Eating disorders are believed to affect predominantly middle-class, intelligent perfectionist young women, often starting at around the age of 17 when conflict with the parents reaches its climax and affects 4% of the population. Anorexics deny feelings of hunger and try to increase energy expenditure by elevated physical activity.

Anorexia and bulimia are believed to be related to obsessive-compulsive personality disorder. When somebody goes on a diet it can disturb a person's brain chemistry, resulting in a loss of control of eating which could trigger an eating disorder.

Marion is 38 and has been anorexic since the age of 17, but she has an obsession with food. She loves to plan and cook meals and enjoys entertaining people with large appetites. She likes to see her guests tuck in heartily to large meals. She herself cleverly disguises the fact that she eats nothing. She is obsessively clean and scrubs her hands meticulously on a regular basis. She has been hospitalised on several occasions and claims to have been 'force fed' during those periods, regarding her body shape on discharge (her correct weight) as grotesque. Within weeks she is as painfully thin as she ever was. Marion has a disgust of fat people, whom she treats with contempt.

Bulimia is the fastest growing eating disorder with 7,000 new cases each year, and it is believed that eating disorders are related to low self-esteem and, like anorexia sufferers, bulimics with their pattern of eating, then vomiting, have a distorted self-image.

Low-fat diets are believed to cause depression by reducing the brain's ability to absorb a substance called serotonin which is an anti-depressant and sleep producer. Stress and anxiety are also related to serotonin levels and people with eating disorders tend to be in a constant state of anxiety as their abnormal food intake alters their brain chemistry, and starvation is believed to reduce anxiety.

It has been speculated that food is a form of sex. Certainly it could be observed that the display, presentation and marketing of food represents "the new pornography".

Post-Traumatic Stress Disorder

Post-traumatic stress disorder is normally associated with war and disaster but can be created by traumas in the everyday environment. Finding a dead body, being involved in, or witnessing a serious road accident, acts of violence or other personal traumas can create an inability to function at the person's previous level. The sufferer will retain the image and emotions associated with the traumatic event and their mind will keep returning to the incident, often to the extent that they will be unable to concentrate on their day to day business.

Somebody suffering from this disorder may avoid places or situations which remind them of the trauma, they may feel guilty that they were unable to intervene in the situation and depression often sets in.

Treatment of post-traumatic stress disorder often involves talking over the traumatic experience with the sufferer in great detail and depth repeatedly until the emotional connections with the memory wear off. The sufferer may even be physically returned to the scene of the incident for the same purpose.

Traumatic amnesia often occurs in times of immense personal and emotional stress when a person may "forget" who they are, where they live and lose memories of their previous life, family and friends. Obviously this is more difficult to investigate, as memory loss may well be invented for personal convenience to avoid responsibilities and problems; however genuine traumatic amnesia is generally recognised in psychological circles.

Depression

Depression of all kinds can be caused by intense inner conflicts which can create guilt feelings. It has also been described as "learned helplessness". Depression is a serious illness and all depressed people should be assessed for the risk of suicide. Depressed people need expert help and often drug treatment. It is not sufficient just to tell a sufferer to snap out of it.

Reactive depression has generally been considered to be a result of adverse circumstances such as a serious financial problems or death and illness in the family, whilst *endogenous* depression has been thought to occur for no apparent reason in a person who has a predisposition to mood disturbance, which may be inherited.

Controversy has existed for a long while as to whether endogenous depression is a separate illness from reactive depression or just a different end of the depression spectrum. It may be that people who are already suffering from a depressive illness find it much harder to cope with adverse life circumstances than people who are not depressed.

The distinction between the two types of a depression can become blurred as the depressive component of manic-depressive psychosis can emerge as a result of stress factors such as bereavement.

Melancholia is a condition characterised by loss of energy, lack of interest in living, listlessness and despair, loss of appetite and wasting, and total disinterest in appearance. The agitated melancholic displays the symptoms of restlessness, is self-accusing, self-injuring and often suicidal.

Many people develop depression at the same time of year and it is felt that it may be related to changes in the seasons specifically the number of daylight hours. This is known as "SAD", Seasonal Affective Disorder, and is helped by the exposure to bright artificial light.

Obsessive-Compulsive Disorder

Obsessive-compulsive disorder is characterised by extreme "ritualistic behaviour" where the person has very rigid behaviour routines which are normally associated with a completely unrealistic fear of dirt and germs which involves obsessional hand washing and exceptionally demanding personal hygiene regimes.

The compulsive person feels a need to carry a task through to a conclusion only to find that when they have finished one task they have to start another. This person is driven by inner energy which can be immensely productive but often drives this person's family to distraction and can affect their health.

People suffering from obsessional disorders start by having an energetic self-willed personality and are over-conscientious in their behaviour. These people tend to have "magical beliefs", for example if the traffic lights are green all the way to work, apart from the obvious sign of a clear road, the obsessional will also construe this as being a "good omen" and that they will not be made redundant. Obsessional disorders can be serious and intractable. A sufferer who is constantly plagued with anti-social thoughts may feel the need to transform these into actions to relieve their tension.

This behaviour is believed to reduce anxiety, as patients prevented from carrying out these regimes become extremely anxious and distressed.

Behaviour therapy can be effective in treating obsessive - compulsive disorder, whereby the therapist will actively prevent the sufferer from acting out his their compulsions.

Obsessions are recognised by the sufferer as being senseless but they are powerless to control them.

Apart from obsessional cleanliness, sufferers may spend hours checking and re-checking gas taps, electric switches and the contents of kitchen drawers to make sure knives have not been left lying around where they could cause harm.

The *"obsessional personality"* is usually a person who is over conscientious and reliable, scrupulous or punctual well beyond average norms. This person may well check and recheck their work to rule out mistakes and live to a very rigid routine which, if disrupted, may create considerable anxiety. These people usually do jobs which require a great deal of attention to detail.

Obsessional neurotics are highly anxious, their anxiety being the main driving force in their lives. Resisting a compulsion can cause acute distress and can only be relieved by carrying out a ritual.

John Bunyan described one of his characters, a priest, as someone who had strong compulsions to mouth sacrilegious words when preaching before his congregation.

Hypochondria is an obsession with illness and the hypochondriac enjoys the attention their "disorders" bring, and revels in the fact that they are incurable.

Alcoholism

It has been debated frequently that many people can use alcohol "recreationally" or "socially" whilst others become addicted, and it has posed the question: do alcoholics have a different make-up from non-alcoholics?

Like father like son?

It is believed that there is a certain gene passed on by alcoholics which is not present in non-alcoholics and psychological observation has witnessed the link between alcoholic fathers and sons.

Alcoholism usually emerges in the late teens and early twenties in males. Around 5% of men and 1% of women from non-alcoholic families are alcoholic, but 20% of sons and 5% of daughters from alcoholic families become alcoholic.

Although this evidence indicates that alcoholism runs in families, some Psychologists believe there might be an "addictive personality type". These people tend not to be able to do anything in moderation, are impulsive and lack self-control. It could be that the effects of alcohol intake resemble the emotional contentment felt by babies when they are being suckled to sleep.

Alcoholism is classed as a behavioural disorder. People often drink to relieve guilt and anxiety, but prolonged drinking actually produces anxiety and depression, insomnia, low mood, irritability and anxiety attacks. Alcoholics have a high rate of divorce, job loss, car accidents and criminality. The death rate for alcoholics is two to three times higher than for non-alcoholics. There are many people who have intolerance to alcohol. These include Orientals, where alcoholism is rare, and white women. Alcoholism causes brain damage – (Korsakoff's syndrome) involving a severe loss of short-term memory.

Children born to women who are heavy drinkers during pregnancy tend to have brain abnormalities and childhood hyperactivity;. this is known as Foetal Alcohol Syndrome. The exposure to alcohol in the womb affects the foetus's central nervous system and creates behavioural problems and low I.Q.

Are there different types of alcoholism?

American social scientist, Professor E M Jellinek, who pioneered the modern scientific approach to alcoholism described five types of alcoholism.

- *Alpha Alcoholism - Type 1.* The drinker has a deep seated psychological problem such as depression or anxiety and they drink excessively to overcome it.

- *Beta Alcoholism - Type 2.* The drinker is not necessarily dependent on alcohol but continual drinking leads to physical and mental depression. This is found particularly in pub landlords.

- *Gamma Alcoholism - Type 3.* This person can go for long periods without drinking but once they start to drink socially they find it impossible to stop. Bingeing on alcohol and then going "on the wagon" is particularly prevalent in Britain and the USA.

- *Delta Alcoholism - Type 4.* The drinker is never really drunk but keeps topping up with alcohol throughout the day.
- *Epsilon Alcoholism - Type 5.* This type afflicts the drinker who only takes alcohol periodically. Their craving is not satisfied until they lose control of themselves and they may finally pass out.

The road to perdition

Very high risk groups for alcoholism are pub landlords and bar staff. Pub landlords are 15 times more likely to be alcoholics than people in "ordinary" jobs and this could be labelled "alcohol seeking behaviour". It could be that these people are already alcoholics and seek employment that satisfies their need to be close to the source of their addiction.

There are 4 stages in the development of alcoholism:

- *The pre-alcoholic phase – Stage 1.* This person drinks to relax on social occasions and to forget worry and anxiety. Larger quantities of alcohol tend to be used to achieve the same effect.

- *The warning phase – Stage 2.* The person suffers loss of memory whilst drunk, indulges in secret drinking and needs to "top up with alcohol" before a social occasion. These people organise their lives around the acquisition of alcohol.

- *The crucial phase – Stage 3.* The person indulges in heavy drinking and experiences hangovers using "hair of the dog" as a remedy. They will drink first thing in the morning, drink alone and neglect food intake. They will experience morning shakes and carry drink around with them. Loss of self control after drinking will be common and their abuse of alcohol will ruin their family and social life. This person will also have strong feelings of self pity.

- *The chronic phase – Stage 4.* The person will consider suicide whilst drinking and be incapable of coping with life. They will go on alcoholic binges, and suffer severe tremors or night sweats. They will get drunk on less alcohol than in the past, and need Dutch courage to cope with life. They will feel unable to give up drinking despite very serious health warnings.

The road to recovery

As a part of a study of alcoholics they were told the negative consequences of their behaviour, i.e. that continuing to drink would damage their health and break up their marriages. This had little effect and the alcoholics made no attempt to sign up for drying-up programmes. In fact, it appears that highlighting the negative consequences of their behaviour tended to have the reverse effect and these people became even more entrenched in their drinking habits.

When the alcoholics had their attention brought to the benefits of signing up for a detoxification programme, i.e. that they would be regarded more favourably by their families and friends and the immediate subject of abstinence was carefully avoided, then a significant number of these people signed up for therapy. This was the first step in cultivating the motivation to stop drinking.

Gerry has been a heavy drinker all his life feeling unable to cope with the problems in life without hitting the bottle. He had successfully managed to conceal his drinking from his wife

Pauline before their marriage. During the period of their marriage his drinking escalated from very heavy social drinking to conceal his sense of low self-esteem when mixing with people, to him his needing a drink in the morning to be able to face the day ahead. Pauline is completely emotionally exhausted, not just with Gerry's drinking but the behaviour that goes with it, which leads to serious marital conflict. Gerry goes on heavy drinking binges, citing his marriage problems as an excuse.

Pauline has threatened divorce on many occasions but her threats have fallen on deaf ears.

A friend offers advice to Pauline telling her to change her tactics. This involves asking Gerry to leave the matrimonial home and then offering to rebuild the marriage on more favourable terms if he is prepared to undergo counselling for his problems. Gerry feels that his marriage is important to him and it is evident that Pauline is not prepared to tolerate his behaviour any more, so is prepared to seek help for his drink problem.

Drug Addiction

Addictive behaviour has been the subject of psychological research for some while. An experiment using rats, in 1954, demonstrated that rats who had electrodes inserted in the "pleasure centre" of the brain, were prepared to run across an electrified grid in order to reach a pedal which they could press to receive further stimulation to this area of the brain.

A substance called dopamine is believed to be responsible for creating the pleasurable sensations people feel when engaged in activities, such as eating and sexual behaviour. It is produced in the brain and many substances increase its production.

174

Drugs such as cocaine and heroin act directly on the pleasure centres of the brain. The constant use of drugs can change the brain chemistry, so more and more of the "pleasurable" substance is required to create the desired effect, and addiction to these substances can occur.

Drug abuse can be a symptom of addictive behaviour. The symptoms of abusing amphetamines (uppers, pep pills) are excitability, sweating, dry mouth and lips, shaking, feelings of persecution, bad breath, insomnia, weight loss, convulsions, dilated pupils and hallucinations. Abusing amphetamines can lead to death.

The symptoms of abusing depressants (sleeping pills, tranquillisers) are a state similar to drunkenness, drowsiness, confusion, slurred speech, trembling and dilated pupils.

Abusing depressants can cause coma and the possibility of death.

The symptoms of abusing narcotics (hard drugs) such as heroin and crack are lethargy, euphoria, drowsiness, constipation, slowed breathing and constricted pupils.

Abusing narcotics can cause convulsions and there is a possibility of death.

There may be a genetic predisposition for drug taking. Any form of drug addiction requires specialist treatment by qualified staff.

Hysteria

The French neurologist, Jean Martin Charcot (a friend of Freud), stated that he believed that the great majority of severe neuroses in women have their origin in the marriage bed.

He believed repressed sexual desires to be the cause of "conversion hysteria" – changes in physical function which stem from distorted instinctual impulses. In other words, psychosomatic illness.

Hysteria can also be classed as a personality disorder. The dominant characteristics of this disorder are shallow unstable emotions, manipulative behaviour and a tendency to over dramatise situations. These people tend to lack self-criticism and display fickle flirtations but have little capacity for sustained personal relationships.

Hysteria was described as a "dissociation" phenomenon by French Psychiatrist Pierre Janet. Dissociation hysteria is displayed by "fugues" (wandering away from one's usual environment with loss of memory, trances and multiple personality). The person who enters into a fugue state is sometimes escaping from an intolerable situation or suffering from severe depression. Often, people commit crimes and blame their "alter ego" for the offences of which they are accused.

Hysteria was called "the vapours" by Victorians and the female womb was blamed. Originally it was believed that the womb wandered around the body causing fainting and convulsions, but later this theory was modified to the notion that noxious vapours could rise up from the womb to the brain and produce symptoms similar to conversion hysteria.

It has been suggested that the capacity for manifesting hysterical symptoms is something which is built into the central nervous system to protect it from overwhelming stress.

Being "hysterical" is common parlance to describe noisy, overdramatic behaviour, but two thirds of patients going to hospital with "hysterical" symptoms are found to have some degree of brain damage.

Hysterical dissociation occurs whenever a certain facet of a person's personality desires to break through into consciousness but is repressed because of the anxiety it would cause. In other words, the living out of two or more separate identities.

A well-balanced personality can express responsibility when the occasion requires it, and when demands and duties are satisfied, relax and become care-free enjoying a party, a fun outing or an evening of sex. In cases of hysterical dissociation the different facets of personality that are usually displayed and acknowledged are kept separate so that the prim and proper person cannot consciously acknowledge the existence of the raunchy other self, and when sexual desire arises the 'puritanical' other self is repressed, no inhibitions on behaviour are exercised and a Jekyll and Hyde personality seems to operate. A Freudian explanation of this phenomenon is that the ego is too weak to cope with moderating the conflicting demands of the Id (basic biological drives) and the Superego (results of parental conditioning). A very much milder from of this is sleepwalking (somnambulism).

Conversion hysteria is a condition where the effects of traumatic psychological experiences render certain parts of the body immobile or malfunctioning. Freud described this condition after observing cases of paralysis and blindness with no apparent physical cause, in soldiers returning from the First World War. He concluded that the shock and horrors of war had had such a traumatic effect on these men, that the action of the mind had created an effect on the body.

Munchausen's Syndrome

Munchausen's syndrome was first described in 1977 by Professor Roy Meadow, a Leeds paediatrician who named it after the German Baron Munchausen, who was known to fake illness because of an abnormal lust for attention. In its advanced stages it is known as Munchausen's Syndrome by Proxy, when the sufferer attempts to be the centre of attention by creating illness in other people. This condition is sometimes observed in mothers who are often observed to be bright and helpful young women and who give the impression of being caring and considerate. However, they deliberately make their child ill. A typical woman is often in her late 20's and suffers some type of eating disorder.

The nurse who killed

In 1993 a young nurse called Beverly Allitt was found guilty of murdering two children and causing grievous bodily harm to three others whilst caring for them as a nurse. This young woman had a history of self-induced injury and shamming illness in an attempt to attract attention. At the time these children were killed and poisoned she was actively the centre of attention in attempts to revive them.

Allitt was convicted in 1993 of the murder of four children and harming nine others. She used insulin injections to cause seizures and often comas in children and potassium injections to bring on convulsions and heart attacks.

She was diagnosed as suffering from Munchausen's Syndrome by Proxy. After creating illness in children she attempted to revive them in front of other nurses and the children's families. This won her what she craved, which was the gratitude of the parents and attention of her colleagues.

It appears that the care Allitt received as a child was given mainly when she hurt herself, possibly creating a link between the experience of personal harm and the expression of love. Munchausen's suffers are believed to have very low self-esteem.

Schizophrenia

Schizophrenia was first identified by Kraeplin in 1902, which he called "dementia praecox" (the senility of youth) and he believed that its symptoms were due to a loss of co-ordination between the intellectual and emotional aspects of the personality. It can begin between the ages of 17 and 30, and although the general understanding of schizophrenia is of a "mad person" plagued by paranoid delusions, it can take different forms.

Paranoid schizophrenia is characterised by the sufferer hearing voices and experiencing delusions and hallucinations of a highly threatening nature. It could be compared to experiencing a nightmare from which the sufferer doesn't wake. The person believes they are being harmed or someone is going to cause them harm.

People with *disorganised (hebephrenic) schizophrenia* experience hallucinations, delusions and disturbances of thought processes. These people can behave in a silly, mischievous, childish and bizarre way. This can turn into aggressive behaviour if the sufferer is acting strangely in response to hallucinations.

Strange physical stances and odd body movements are displayed by *catatonic schizophrenics* and their behaviour can include odd physical movements and complete immobility for hours on end.

Simple schizophrenia is characterised by social deterioration and appearance during the late teens and early 20's. The sufferer can become apathetic, have difficulty making friends and find it difficult to continue with their studies or hold down a job. Often these people drop out of society and become tramps and drifters. People who develop schizophrenia are believed to inherit a vulnerability to exhibit schizoid symptoms, which are believed to be triggered by environmental stresses which activate the genetic predisposition. Some 1% of the population will be hospitalised with schizophrenia at some point in their lives.

A Psychiatrist called Schneider, in 1959, detailed the "first rank symptoms of schizophrenia" which affects 1% of the population.

Thoughts, emotions, impulses and actions are experienced as under external or alien control. The sufferers can also believe that their minds are controlled by an outside force. They may think their thoughts are broadcast to Martians, the Communists and 'The Government'. Voices may be heard discussing one's thoughts and behaviour or are heard arguing about the sufferer referring to them by name. The sufferer may experience false delusions, i.e. they may think they are Jesus or Napoleon, or experience delusions of persecution, i.e. that they are being poisoned.

Other major symptoms of the illness were later identified described in 1969. Thought disorders are characterised by an inability to keep to the point and the sufferer often uses similar sounding words to the ones he needs but which have a different meaning. Often an apparently incoherent jumble of words is produced.

The schizophrenic is likely to display insensitivity, lack of consideration and indifference to other people's feelings. They may react in a completely inappropriate way to emotionally charged information; such as laughing at bad news or getting angry without any apparent reason. Sudden mood changes may well be in evidence. There is also an inability to make decisions or carry out a particular activity, a loss of interest in life and affection for loved ones.

Schizophrenics experience a certain kind of mental insecurity whereby everyday events may well threaten their very existence.

They fear *engulfment*, which is a dread of being swallowed up by others if involvement becomes too close. To be loved is more threatening than being hated; they see love as a form of hate.

They fear *implosion*, they feel empty like a vacuum and anything which can threaten their empty space must be protected at all costs.

They fear *petrification* or *depersonalisation*, which is a fear of being turned into stone, or turning others into stone, or becoming a robot, that is, having their thoughts controlled.

Modern science has discovered chemical malfunctions in the brains of schizophrenics – an overabundance of the chemical dopamine. People who suffer from Parkinson's disease have a deficiency of this chemical, and when they have their dopamine levels increased with drug treatment they can often display the symptoms of schizophrenia, i.e. paranoia, hallucinations and delusions. Schizophrenics who have their dopamine levels reduced by drug treatment can display the symptoms of Parkinson's disease, i.e. trembling of limbs and speech difficulties.

(Dopamine is produced from a chemical chain reaction starting with adrenalin, the stress hormone).

An eminent Psychiatrist called R.D. Laing claimed that schizophrenia could only be understood as something which takes place *between* people and not inside them, and particularly that this related to interactions within the family, and created *"The Family Interaction Model"* of schizophrenia. In their book *"Sanity, Madness and the Family"* in 1964, R.D. Laing and A.Esterton looked at eleven family case histories. In all these families there was a schizophrenic member. Laing felt that dysfunctional family interactions created schizophrenia in family members.

Gregory Bateson, in 1956, investigated families that had schizophrenic members and found that these families did indeed have abnormal patterns of communication which mainly took the form of contradictory messages relating to emotional dependency.

Gavin's parents have always had difficulty communicating both with each other and with Gavin; often Gavin's mother will say something and then deny it later. Gavin is 21 and trying to establish some independence. His mother, has for a long while, complained that he doesn't do anything for himself yet she insists on doing everything for him (double-bind). She puts her arms around him and at the same time calls him "baby", as if despising him for being so emotionally dependeant (another double-bind).

His father sees him as being babied and resents the amount of time his wife devotes to running Gavin's life and becomes hostile to Gavin. Gavin's father is something of a control freak himself and rules Gavin's life in a strong authoritarian manner, whilst at the same time saying he is incapable of making decisions for himself (yet another double-bind). His mother feels his father is too strict.

All the conflicting patterns of behaviour then in turn cause problems between the parents, which exacerbate the friction within the family. Gavin is in a quandary about whose side to take when his parents are arguing. Gavin is the prime victim of these dysfunctional communication patterns and starts to suffer severe neurotic symptoms which over a period of time progress into a paranoid illness.

Gavin becomes hostile to and suspicious of people around him. He starts to believe that his thoughts are being controlled and that the devil is talking to him through television newsreaders.

Gavin's girlfriend understands how to manage his illness, by being sympathetic to his delusions, but not encouraging them. She notices that if she dismisses Gavin's delusions he can become aggressive. Gavin's girlfriend arranges for him to have expert psychiatric help for this very serious illness.

Manic-Depressive Disorder

Manic-depressive disorder is a condition where the sufferer's behaviour fluctuates between euphoria and deep depression.

The state of euphoria is a highly elated mood where a person feels they can take on the world and have unrealistic goals of achievement. The sufferer feels they have a great deal of energy and rushes wildly around without actually achieving anything and many of their social inhibitions such as sexual control may break down. They may go on a wild spending spree, running up massive debts, take on crazy business projects, have little need for sleep and have exaggerated ideas of their own importance. This behaviour then gives way to acute depression where the sufferer has a deep sense of despair, feeling of ugliness, hopelessness, withdrawal from life and they can often be suicidal.

183

There appears to be an inherited proneness to this disorder, which is a very serious psychiatric illness treatable only by Psychiatrists with drugs.

Is mental illness real?

R.D.Laing and Thomas Szaz claimed mental illness is a myth and that so-called mentally ill people just have behaviour problems that deviate from the norm.

In 1973 David Rosenhan of Stanford University tested the criteria for diagnosing mental illness when he arranged for eight "normal" people to be admitted to a psychiatric hospital on the basis that they claimed to be hearing voices. On the ward they behaved in a reasonably normal manner. These fake patients included a psychology graduate, a Psychiatrist, three Psychologists and a journalist.

The genuine patients in the hospital were convinced of the sanity of the fake patients whom they suspected were researchers, whilst very few of the medical staff believed the fake patients to be sane and some of them were discharged with the diagnosis of "schizophrenia in remission".

Much of what is accepted as normal and sane is dependent upon the culture in which the individual lives. Very many people in different countries have customs which would seem peculiar by our standards, but are considered normal for where they live.

It is believed that in some Muslim societies it is the accepted norm for women committing adultery to be stoned to death and that in Taiwan a woman may cut off her husband's penis if found consorting with other women. In some African tribes there is a strong belief in the "Tokoloshi man", a small monkey-like creature with one buttock and a huge penis which is thrown over his shoulder. Such is the belief in this creature that certain tribes people sleep three feet above the ground to escape his attentions. Many religious people claim to have received messages from God instructing them on how to conduct their lives.

However, there is no doubt that when somebody's behaviour deviates severely from the "norm", particularly if they have paranoid delusions, this can create a threat to the safety and structure of the family and society.

Creativity

Dr Felix Post, by examining the biographies of famous men, claims that creativity is linked to psychiatric, psychosexual and personality disorders.

Compared to 17% of politicians and 18% of scientists, 37% of painters and 46% of writers studied appear to have had psychiatric problems. These include D.H. Lawrence, Proust, Tolstoy, Van Gogh, Picasso and Turner. It appears that 72% of novelists and playwrights suffered from depressive conditions. The phenomenon of cause and effect may come into play here. Obviously if an author, painter or composer invests a significant amount of their personality, as a full-time occupation, into producing works of art to poor critical acclaim, then this is likely to have a detrimental affect on their psychological well being.

Therapies

Essentially the first step in seeking help for any type of mental health problem is consultation with a general practitioner and, if necessary, subsequent referral to a Clinical Psychologist with the

185

National Health Service. Some Clinical Psychologists also work in private practice.

The other therapies detailed and described are available in the private sector and people who believe they need assistance with psychological problems should always consult with clinically qualified staff before pursuing complementary therapies.

The aims of psychotherapy in general are to help the patient get rid of intense and unrealistic fears. It helps the patient learn and establish new ways of behaving and interacting with other people and to achieve greater self-knowledge. The general consensus of opinion is that at least half the number of people who receive psychotherapy feel an improvement afterwards.

Group therapy consists of group discussion of personal problems under the guidance of a therapist. The members of the group can treat each other. The idea is that a person suffering from a nervous disorder should understand that they are not alone and that other people have feelings they can relate to and who can show real empathy for them. These groups also serve as social skills learning situations as other group members can correct each other's undesirable traits enabling them to obtain better social interactions in their daily lives.

Client-centred therapy, (devised by Carl Rogers in the 1940's), involves the therapist listening to their patients' problems in a non-judgemental way in an attempt to create good self-esteem.

The "Rorschach" inkblot test can reveal both a person's personality and intelligence. The subject is shown ten inkblots one at a time and asked to describe what they see. The person can turn the inkblot into different positions: (these inkblots were created by the author).

186

Rorschach type inkblots

Different interpretations of these inkblots could be a butterfly, a bat, people or parts of the anatomy. They can be perceived as innocent or threatening depending on the personality make-up of the viewer.

Scoring of this test is fairly standardised, but general assessments of the interpretations are made at the discretion of the Psychologist conducting the tests. It is possible to differentiate between normal and psychotic individuals and even distinguish between different types of psychotics.

Art therapy originates from Jungian psychology and the therapist may ask the patient to express their innermost thoughts and feelings by painting and drawing. The circle is symbolic of the self and abstract designs, and involves drawing circles and designs within them. These are useful in assessing a patient's state of mind, feelings and emotions. The art therapist may also ask the patient to make pictures of their dreams.

Transactional analysis was devised by Byrne in 1968 and states that an individual will have three ego states: the parent, the adult and the child. Sometimes the child comes to the forefront of personality and sometimes it is the adult. The healthy personality is one where the parent ego state is in control and indulges the adult whilst keeping a tight rein on the child. The aim of this therapy is to readjust faulty functioning of these ego states to achieve a more harmonious personality.

Arthur Janov, in 1970, developed 'Primal Therapy' whereby maladaptive or neurotic behaviour is believed to relate to traumas caused at or during one's birth and is a result of bottling up pains and tensions emanating experienced in early life. Therapy involves re-living these experiences so that they can be managed.

Gestalt therapy developed by Perls in 1969 aims to help people become "whole" by putting them in touch with their entire selves and their surroundings.

Other therapists can be either Freudian or Jungian. Freudian therapists often concentrate on probing the subconscious mind looking for traumatic childhood experiences as a cause of the nervous disorder. They may focus mainly on biological themes such as sex. Jungian therapy is more concerned with a person's spiritual needs.

Analytical Hypnotherapy can use Freudian and Jungian psychoanalytic techniques. Hypnosis is believed to aid "catharsis" (the release of nervous tension). The release of the traumatising memories creates an "abreaction" (a re-experience of the memory and the emotion associated with it). This is believed to be a much more rapid and painless form of psychoanalysis and a reputable practitioner should be found.

Andy is 28 years old and has a string of very unsuccessful relationships with women, all of which lack emotional satisfaction.

He feels that his chances of ever settling down in a long term relationship are remote as his sexual partners claim he is cold and aloof during sexual relations and he is unable to express any warmth.

Andy's parents have gone through some very bad patches during the period of their marriage and Andy perceives that their problems have had a bad effect on him.

He consults a therapist in an attempt to find a solution to his problems. The therapist invites Andy, under hypnosis (a method originally used by Freud) to discuss his "presenting problem" – i.e. the problem of unsatisfactory relationships with women and his parents' marriage problems, which he does at some length.

The therapist then regresses Andy to adolescence in an attempt to create a "catharsis" – a release of guilt and emotional distress. Over a number of sessions Andy discusses his adolescent experiences with his therapist, and, as she expects to she obtains a confession.

At the age of 15 Andy and his best friend indulged in mutual masturbation to orgasm. Andy has always had a deep-seated fear that he is homosexual because of this experience. He feels guilty and ashamed of what he did but also remembers the physical pleasure he felt. This has acted as an emotional restraint on his relationships with women. He subconsciously wonders whether people suspect his "guilty secret" when they are in his company and whether they think he is gay.

The therapist has been very skilful in obtaining this information and achieving an abreaction. She keeps Andy in hypnosis, giving him positive suggestions for his well-being. He has experienced

189

an intense and profound emotional release from his psychological tensions and guilt – catharsis.

Andy then goes on to make a successful heterosexual relationship with a woman.

Many mental health professionals believe that acting may serve as an externalisation of hidden psychic dramas by which we can release our repressed anxieties, conflicts and tensions. Navaho Indians use ceremonial dramas to cure people with psychological and physical disorders.

In some psychiatric hospitals, drama therapy is used and patients are required to act out different social roles which are then videotaped, shown back to the patient and then used as a basis for improving that person's social skills.

Carl Gustav Jung described anxiety as a malaise which affects the human race. Most people suffer mild anxieties which do not interfere with their functioning in everyday life.

Psychological disorder can result from what Freud described as 'common unhappiness'.

Happiness is probably a difficult concept to define. Positive feelings about ourselves and our lives are obviously necessary ingredients for happiness particularly where they are combined with optimistic prospects for the future.

"Remember this, that very little is needed to make a happy life"
Marcus Aurelius Antonious – Roman Emperor (121-80)

REFERENCES

Apes & Us

Bryson W (2003) "A Short History of Nearly Everything" Doubleday London.

Daily Mail 2002

Fouts RS, Fouts DH, a Schoenfield D (1984) "Sign Language – Conversational Interactions between Chimpanzees. Sign Language Studies 341-12

Gardner RA & Gardner RT (1978) Comparative Psychology and Language Acquisition – "Psychology – The State of the Art" Annals of the New York Academy of Sciences 309 37 – 76

Johanson Donald & Blake Edgar "From Lucy to Language" London Weidenfeld & Nicholson 2001

Jensen AR (1969) "How much can we boost IQ and Scholastic Achievement?" Harvard Educational Review 39 1-123

Lander E Director of the Whitehead Institute/Massachusetts Institute of Technology Centre for Genome Research

LeFarge S

Lewis J "Anthropology Made Simple" Oxford

PBS Nova "In Search of Human Origins" first broadcast 1999

Scientific American "An Ancestor to Call Our Own" January 2003 p54 - 63

Sykes Bryan "The Seven Daughters of Eve" London Bantam Press 2001

Terrence HS "Nim" New York AA Knopf (1979)

Wilson Alan 1987

Our Personality Traits

Adler AC (1936) "The Neurotic's Picture of the World" International Journal of Psychology. New York. Harcourt Brace Jarovich

Adorno TW et al (1950) "The Authoritarian Personality" New York Harper Row

Aristotle

Bem SL (1974) "The measurement of psychological androgyny" Journal of Consulting and Clinical Psychology 42(2) 155-62

Bijon JN "Promoting optimum Learning in Children" Hodder & Stoughton 1976

Blakemore C (1988) "The Mind Machine" London: BBC Publications

Blair RJR, Jones L, Clarke F, & Smith M (1997) The Psychopathic Individual: A Lack of Responsiveness to Distress Cues? Psychophysiology 34 192-198

Damasio AR (1994) Descartes' Error. Emotion Rationality and the Human Brain. New York, GP Putnam & Sons

192

Eysenck HJ (1977) "Crime and Personality" Routledge & Kegan Paul

Eysenck HJ(Ed) "A Model for Personality" New York, Springer (1980)

Eysenck HJ & Eysenck MW "Personality and Individual Differences" (London 1985)

Eysenck HJ "Biological Basis of Personality" (Springfield Illinois 1967)

Eysenck HJ(Ed) "Readings in Extraversion – Introversion" 3 Vols. (London 1970)

Freud S (1976) "The Psychopathology of Everyday Life" Pelican Freud library (5) Harmondsworth, Middlesex, Penguin (original work published 1901)

Freud S (1977) "Three Essays on the Theory of Sexuality" Pelican Freud Library (7) Harmondsworth, Middlesex, Penguin (Original work published 1905)

Freud S (1984) "Beyond the Pleasure Principle" Pelican Freud Library (11) Harmondsworth, Middlesex, Penguin (Original work published 1922)

Freud S (1984) "The Ego and the Id" Pelican Freud Library (11) Harmondsworth, Middlesex, Penguin (Original work published 1923)

Galen C (2AD) Kuhn (G Led) (1821-33) Opera omnia (The only complete edition of Galen's surviving works)

Gall, Franz Joseph (1758 – 1828)

Godda Luigi, Director of the Gregor Mendel Institute Rome

Goffman E (1971) "The Presentation of Self in Everyday Life" Harmondsworth, Middlesex, Penguin

Hart RD (1996) "Psychopathy: A clinical construct whose time has come" Criminal Justice and Behaviour 23, 25-54

Inbau FE "Lie Detection and Criminal Interrogation: Baltimore Williams and Watkins (1942) pp 60-70

Jensen AR (1969) How much can we boost IQ and Scholastic Achievement

Jung CG (1953 – 71) "Collected Works" London

Jung CG (1959) "The Archetypes and the Collective Unconscious" Routledge & Kegan Paul London

Jung CG (1964) "Man and his Symbols" London Aldus Jupiter Books

Kretschner E (1936) "Physique and Character" 2nd ed (WJH Sprott & K Paul French trans) New York Trubner

Lavator John

Le Doux J (1998) "The Emotional Brain" London Weidenfeld & Nicholson

Leibniz GWF von: Broad CD: Liebniz: an Introduction Cambridge

Lombrosso

Lykken DT (1957) "A study of anxiety in the sociopathic personality" Journal of Abnormal and Social Psychology 556 – 10

Maslow A (1968) "Towards a Psychology of Being" (2nd ed) New York Van Nostrand – Reinhold

Morris D (1967) "The Naked Ape" London Jonathan Cape
(1969) "The Human Zoo" London Jonathan Cape
(1977) "Manwatching" London

Nietzsche F "Also Sprach Zarathustra"

Patrick CJ (1994) "Emotion and Psychopathy: Startling new insights. Psychophysiology 31 319-335

Schneider K (trans Hamilton MW 1958) Psychopathic Personalities Bristol

Sagan E (1988) "Freud Women and Morality": Basic Books Inc NY

Sheldon William

Watson JB (1967) Behaviour: An Introduction to Comparative Psychology with an Introduction by RJ Herrstein – New York

How we get on with other people: Strangers and Families

Asch SE (1951) "Effect of group pressure upon the modification and distortion of judgements" In H Guetzkow (Ed) Groups Leadership and Men. Pittsburgh, Pennsylvania: Carnegie Press.

Asch SE (1956) "Studies of independence and submission to group pressure: A minority of one against a unanimous majority." Psychological Monographs 70(9) (whole no 416)

Berscheid E & Walster "Physical Attractiveness" Advances in Experimental Social Psychology, Vol. 7, London, Academic Press

Byrne D (1971) "The Attraction Paradigm" Academic Press New York

Byrne D (1973) "Interpersonal Attraction" Annual Review of Psychology 24 317 – 36

Crime and the Family 1993

Crutchfield RS (1955) "Conformity and Character" American Psychologist 10, 191 – 8

Darley JM & Latané B "Bystander Intervention in Emergencies: Diffusion of Responsibility" Journey of Personality and Social Psychology 8 377 – 383 (1968)

Efran MA "The effect of physical appearance on the judgement of guilt, interpersonal attraction and severity of recommended punishment in a simulated jury task" Journal of Research into Personality 8, 45 – 54 (1974)

Erikson Milton (1968) "The Inhumanity of Ordinary People" International Journal of Psychiatry 6 p278 - 9

Festinger L (1957) "A Theory of Cognitive Dissonance" New York – Harper Row

Haley J (1964) "Research on Family Patterns: an instrument measurement" Family Process

Hildreth et al (1971)

Jourard SM (1966) "An exploratory study of body accessibility" British Journal of Social and Clinical Psychology 221 – 31

Laing RD & Esterton A (1964) "Sanity Madness and the Family."

Laing RD (1965) "The Divided Self" Penguin Harmondsworth Middlesex

Laing RD (1971) "The Politics of the Family" London

Latané B & Darley JM "The Unresponsive Bystander: Why doesn't he help?" London Appleton – Century – Crofts (1970)

La Pierre RT (1934) "Attitudes versus Actions" Social Forces 13 230 – 7

Milgram (1974) "Obedience to Authority" NY Harper Row

Morris D, Colle P, Marsh P & O'Shaughnessy M (1979) Gestures London

Scheflen A E "How Behaviour Means" Garden City NY Anchor Press – Doubleday (1974)

Scheflen (1964) "The Significance of posture in communication systems" Psychiatry 27 316 – 31

Sherif (1936) "The Psychology of Social Norms" New York Harper Row

Watson ON & Graves TD (1966) "Quantitative Research on proxemic behaviour."

Zimbardo PG (1973) "On the ethics of intervention in human psychological research with specific reference to the Stanford Prison experiment. Cognition 2 (2) 243 – 55

Our Loves Marriages & Divorces

Aaron Arthur (Pennsylvania State University)

Argyle M Henderson MC (1984) "The rules of friendship" Journal of Social and Personal Relationships (1) 209-35

Athanasiou R & Sarkin R (1974) "Premarital sexual behaviour and post-marital adjustment" Archives of sexual behaviour" (3) 207-25

Bentler PM & Newcomb MD (1978) "Longitudinal study of marital success and failure" Journal of Consulting and Clinical Psychology (46) 1053-70

Bernard J (1972) The Future Of Marriage, World: New York

Birchler GR (1972) "Differential patterns of instrumental affilliative behaviours as a function of degree in marital distress and level of intimacy." PhD dissertation University of Oregon

Bloom B, Asher S J & White S W (1978) Marital Disruption as a stressor. A Review and analysis, Psychological Bulletin (85) 867-94

Byrne D (1971) "The Attraction Paradigm" Academic Press: New York

Cole C A (1976) 'A Behavioural analysis of married and living together couples' Unpublished PhD dissertation University of Houston Tx

Crawley News 2004

Darwin C "The Origin of Species" JM Dent & Sons Ltd

Dindia K & Fitzpatrick MA (1985) "Marital Communication; three approaches compared". In SW Duck & D Perlman (Eds) "Understanding Personal Relationships" Sage, London

Duck S W "Human Relationships" (1986) Sage, London

Duck S W (1984b) "Personal Relationships 5: Repairing Personal Relationships" Academic Press, London & New York

Fitzpatrick MAC (1977) "A typographical approach to communication in relationships" in B Ruben (EdEd) Communication Yearbook 1 Transaction Press, New Jersey

Fitzpatrick MA & Badzinski D (1985) "All in the family" in GR Miller & ML Knapp (Eds) Handbook of Interpersonal Communication. Sage, Beverly Hills, CA

Furstenberg FF (1979) "Premarital Pregnancy & Marital Instability. In G Levinger & OC Moles (Eds) Divorce and Separation, Basic Books: New York

Goffman J (1979) "Beyond jealousy and possessiveness". In G Clanton & L Smith (Eds) Jealousy, Prentice Hall, Englewood Cliffs, NJ

Goffman J (1979) "Empirical Investigations of Marriage" Academic Press, New York

Hendrick C, Hendrick S, Foote F & Slapion-Foote MC (1984) "Do men and women love differently?" Journal of Social and Personal Relationships (1) 177-96

Hetherington EM (1979)"Divorce: a child's perspective" American Psychologist (34) 851-58

Huston et al (1981) "From courtship to marriage, mate selection as an interpersonal process" SW Duck & R Gilman (Eds) Personal Relationships 2: developing personal relationships. Academic Press, London, New York

Kelly C, Huston TL & Cate RM (1985) "Premarital relationships correlates of the erosion of satisfaction in marriage" Journal of Social & Personal Relationships (2) 167-78

Lee JA (1973) "The Colors of Love" An exploration of the ways of loving. New Press, Ontario

Levinger G (Univ of Mass.) USA

Lips HM & Morrison A (1986) "Changes in the sense of family amongst couples having their first child" Journal of Social and Personal Relationships

Mazur R (1977) "Beyond jealousy and possessiveness" In G Clanton & L Smith (Eds) "Jealousy" Prentice Hall, Englewood Cliffs, NJ

Morris D "The Naked Ape" (1977) London, Jonathan Cape

Morris D "The Human Zoo" (1977) London Jonathan Cape

Morris D "Manwatching" London

Mott FL & Moore SF (1979) "The Causes of Marital Disruption Among Young American Women: An Inter-Disciplinary Perspective." Journal of Marriage and the Family (41) 335-65

Murstein BI & Glaudin VC (1968) "The use of MMPI in the determination of marital adjustment" Journal of Marriage and the Family (30) 651-5

Noller P (1982) "Channel consistency and inconsistency in the communication of married couples" Journal of Personality and Social Psychology (43) 732-41

Rausch HL, Barry WA, Hertel RK, & Swain MA, (1974) "Communication, Conflict & Marriage" Jossey-Bass, San Francisco

Renne KS (1970) "Correlates of dissatisfaction in marriage" Journal of Marriage and the Family (32) 54-67

Riskin J & Faunce EE (1972) "An evaluative review of family interaction research" Family Processes (11) 365-455

Rollins BC & Feldman H (1970) "Marital satisfaction over the life cycle" Journals of Marriage and the Family (32) 20-8

Rubin B R (1971) "The role of content information seeking and impression formation" Communication Monographs (44) 81-90

Rubin Z (Harvard University) "Measurement of Romantic Love" Journal of Personality and Social Psychology (1970) VolVol. 16 (No 2) p265-73

Rubin Z (1973) "Liking and Loving" Holt Rinehard and Winston, NY

Shettel-Neuber J et al "Physical Attractiveness of the other person" and "Jealousy" Personality & Social Psychology Bulletin

Weiss RS "The Emotional Impact of Marital Separation" Journal of Social Issues 1976 v32 p135-45

Our Sex Lives

Darwin C "The Origin of Species" JM Dent & Sons

Donnerstein Edward & Barrett Gary, Iowa State University – "Effects of Erotic Stimuli on Male Aggression Towards Females" Journal of Personality and Social Psychology 1978 volVol. 36 No2 p180

Freud S "Introductory Lectures on Psychoanalysis" Vols 1&2 (1973) Pelican Freud Library, Penguin Harmondsworth

Freud (1977a) "Three Essays on the Theory of Sexuality" Pelican Freud (7) Harmondsworth, Middlesex, Penguin (original work published 1905)

Kinsey AC Pomeroy WB & Martin CE (1948) "Sexual Behaviour in the Human Female"

Masters WH & Johnson (1966) "Human Sexual Response" London

Mead M (1935) "Sex and Temperament in Three Primitive Societies" NY

Morokoff Patricia J "Uniformed Services" University of the Health Sciences (Department of Defence) "Effects of Sex, Guilt, Repression, Sexual Arousability and Sexual Experience on Female Sexual Arousal during Erotica and Fantasy. "Journal of Personality & Society Psychology" 1985 volVol.49 Vol p177 – 87

Morris D (1967) "The Naked Ape" London, Jonathan Cape

Morris D (1967) "The Human Zoo" London, Jonathan Cape

Morris D (1977) "Manwatching" London

Peplau Letitia Anne: University of California. Los Angles. "Research on Homosexual Couples: An overview" Journal of Homosexuality. Winter 1982 vVol.8 No2 p3-8

Sagan E (1988) "Freud Women and Morality" Basic Books Inc.

University of California

US Cancer Institute

Everyday Life

Adorno et al (1950) "The Authoritarian Personality" New York Harper & Row

Allport GW (1954) "The Nature of Prejudice" Reading, Massachusetts Addison Wesley

Argyle MC (1989) "The Social Psychology of Work" (2nd ed)

Bandura A, Ross D & Ross SA (1963) "Imitation of film – mediated aggressive models – Journal of Abnormal and Social Psychology 66 3-11

Bradburn (1969) "The Structure of Psychological Well-being" Aldine NY

Cannon WB (1929) "Bodily changes in pain, hunger, fear and rage" New York Appleton-Century-Crofts

Cannon WB (1929) "The James-Lange theory of emotions; a critical examination and an alternative theory. American Journal of Psychology (39) 106-24

Check J, Perlman D & Malamuth N (1985) "Loneliness and aggressive behaviour" Journal of Social and Personal Relationships (2) 243-52

Dutton DC & Aron AP (1974) "Some evidence for heightened sexual attraction under conditions of high anxiety" Journal of Personality and Social Psychology (30) 510-17

Eron L & Huesman R, University of Illinois reported in "Class Bully more likely to break laws as an Adult" Centre Daily Times (State College PA) August 17, 1983

Freud S "The Psychopathology of Everyday Life" Pelican Freud Library (5) Harmondsworth Middlesex, Penguin (Original work published 1905)

Holmes TH & Rahe RH (1967) "The Social Readjustment Rating Scales" Journal of Psychosomatic Research II 213-18

Howells K "Social Relationships in Violent Offenders" Personal Relationships, Academic Press London & New York

Jones et al (1985) "Relational Stress: an analysis of situations and events associated with loneliness" In SW Duck & D Perlman (Eds) Understanding Personal Relationships, Sage: London

Jenkins CD (1971) "Psychological and Social precursors of Coronary Disease – New England Journal of Medicine (284) 244-5 30 1-16

Kohlberg L (1976) Moral Stages & Moralization, In T Likana (Ed) Moral Development & Behaviour NY Holt

Larson F et al (1982) "Time alone in daily experience" in LA Peplau and D Perlman (Eds) Loneliness. A sourcebook of Current Theory, Research and Therapy, Wiley, Interscience, New York

Lewin K, Lippitt R & White R (1939) "Patterns of aggressive behaviour in experimentally created "social climates" Journal of Social Psychology 10 271-99

Lorenz KZ (1966) "On Aggression" London, Methuen

Machiavelli, Niccollo

Megargee EI (1966) "Uncontrolled and Overcontrolled personality types in extreme antisocial aggression". Psychological Monographs – General and Applied (Whole No 611)

Parke et al (1977) "Some effects of violent and non-violent movies on the behaviour of juvenile delinquents in L Berkowitz (Ed). Advances in experimental psychology Vol 10 NY Academic Press

Perlman D & Peplau LA (1981) "Loneliness" In SW Duck & R Gilmour (Eds) Personal Relationships 3, Personal Relationships in Disorder. Academic Press London & New York

Peplau LA & Perlman D (Eds) (1982) Loneliness: A Source book of Current Theory – Research and Therapy, Wiley, Interscience NY (1981)

Rook KS (1984) "Interventions for loneliness: a reviewed analysis". In LA Peplau & SE Goldston (Eds) Loneliness: a current Sourcebook of Theory Research and Therapy, Wiley, Interscience NY

Sagan E (1988) "Freud Women and Morality" Basic Books Inc NY

Schacter S & Singer J (1962) "Cognitive social and psychological determinants of emotional states: Psychological Review (69) 379-99

Schacter 1971

Seyle (1956) "The Stress of Life" McGraw Hill, New York

Stein, Steven J PhD and Book, Howard EMD "Emotional Intelligence" (2000) Stoddart Publishing Co, Canada

Tunstall J (1967) "Old and Alone" Humanities Press, New York

University of New Orleans
Weiss Robert University of Massachusetts

Yorkshire Centre for Eating Disorders

Our Life Stages

Annals of the American Academy of Political and Social Science 464 120-31

Atchley RC (1982) "Retirement, leaving the world of work"

Bradburn (1969) "The Structure of Psychological well-being" Aldine NY

Burton R "Anatomy of Melancholy"

Erikson E (1980) "Identity and the Life Cycle" NY Norton

Jung CG (1953-71) Collected Works London

Kubler Ross E (1969) "On Death and Dying" Macmillan NY

Krupp (1962)

Parkes C M (1970) The First Year of Bereavement: a longitudinal study of the reaction of London widows to the death of their husbands. Psychiatry 33, 444-67

Readers Digest Family Medical Advisor, Readers Digest Association, London

Ramsay & de Groot (Nine Stages of Grief)

Raphael B (1984) "The Anatomy of Bereavement" London, Hutchinson

Storr A (1973) Jung London (Fontana Modern Masters Series)

Stroebe W & Stroebe M (1983) "Who suffers more? Sex differences in health risk of the widowed." Psychological Bulletin (93) 279-301

Twain, Mark

Sleeping and The Dreams We Have

Aristotle

Blakemore (1988) "The mind machine" London BBC Publications

Caton R

Dement & Kleitman (1957) "The relation of eye movements during sleep to dream activity. An objective method for the study of dreaming". Journal of Experimental Psychology 53 (5) 339-46

Freud S "Introductory Lectures on Psychoanalysis" VolVol. 1 Pelican, Freud Library (1973) Penguin Harmondsworth

Freud S (1976) "The Interpretation of Dreams" Pelican Freud Library (4) Harmondsworth, Middlesex: Penguin (original work published in 1900)

Jung CG (1963) "Memories, Dreams and Reflections" London Collins RKP

Oswald I (1974) "Sleep" Penguin, Harmondsworth, Middlesex, 2nd ed

Plato

Scherner KA

Some Problems With Our Mental Health & Therapies Which May Help

Bateson et al (1956) "Towards a theory of schizophrenia" In Steps to an Ecology of Mind

Berne (1968) "Games people play" Harmondsworth, Middlesex

Bowlby JC (1951) "Maternal Care and Mental Health" Geneva World Organisation

Bunyan, John

Charcot, Jean Martin

Fairburn WRD (1952) "A revised psychopathology of psychoses and psychoneuroses". In psychoanalytic studies of the personality.

Freeman D & Garety PA (2004) Paranoia: The psychology of Persecutory Delusions, Hove, Psychology Press

Guardian (1993)

Gross, Richard D "Psychology: The Science of Mind and Behaviour" Hodder and Stoughton, London

Gull, William

Iversen (1979) "The Chemistry of the Brain" Scientific American 24, 134-49

Janet, Pierre

Janov A (1973) "The Primal Scream" London Abacus

Jellinek E M Prof: USA

Jung CA (1953-71) "Collected Works" London

Kalant H "Readings from the Encyclopaedia of Neuroscience" 1989

Kendall RE (1976) "The classification of depression: a review of contemporary confusion" British Journal of Psychiatry 129 15-28

Keys W University of Pittsburgh

Kraeplin E (1913) Psychiatry (8th ed) Leipzig: Thieme

Kraupl Taylor F (1979) "Psychopathology: its causes and symptoms "Rev edn, Sunbury-on-Thames

Laing RD & Esterton A (1964) "Sanity, Madness and the Family"

Laing RD & Esterton A (1965) "The Divided Self" Penguin, Harmondsworth, Middlesex

Lewis AJ (1967) "Problems of Obsessional Illness" and "Obsessional Illness" In Inquiries into Psychiatry, London

Marks (1981)

McArdle

Meadow Prof. Roy Leeds, Paediatrician

Mereno JL (1953) "Who Shall Survive?" (2nd ed) New York Beacon

Maudsley Hospital

Perls FS (1969) "Gestalt Therapy Verbatim" New York

Pinel, Phillip

Post, Dr Felix

Rogers CR (1951) "Client-centred therapy, its current practices, implications and theory" Boston, Houghton, Mifflin

Rosenhan DL "On being sane in insane places". Science 179, 250-258 (1973)

Rorshach H

Schneider K (trans Hamilton MW 1958) "Psychopathic Personalities" London

Schneider K (1959) "Primary and Secondary Symptoms in Schizophrenia". In SR Hirsh and MM Sheppard (Eds) (1974) "Themes and Variations in European Psychiatry" New York, John Wright

Seligman MEP (1975) "Helplessness: on depression, development and death" San Francisco, WH Freedman

Slater E & Roth M (1977) "Clinical Psychiatry" (3rd edn) London Balliere, Tindall and Cassell

Szaz (1972) "The myth of mental illness" London, Palladin

Whitlock FA (1967) "The aetiology of hysteria" Acta Psych Scand 43a 44

Wolpe J (1958) "Psychotherapy by Reciprocal Inhibition"

Subject Index